KIDS COMPUTER CREATIONS

USING YOUR COMPUTER FOR ART & CRAFT FUN

Carol Sabbeth

illustrations by
Loretta Trezzo Braren

WILLIAMSON PUBLISHING • CHARLOTTE, VERMONT

Library of Congress
Cataloging-in-Publication Data

Sabbeth, Carol, 1957-
    Kids' computer creations: using your
computer for art & craft fun/ Carol Sabbeth
        p.   cm.
    Includes index.
    ISBN 0-913589-92-6
    1. Handicraft—Data processing—Juvenile
literature. 2. Creative activities and seat
work—Juvenile literature. [1. Computer art.
2. Handicraft.] I. Title.
TT149.515   1995
    745.5—dc20   94-44240
                                    CIP
                                    AC

Cover design: Trezzo-Braren Studio
Interior design: Trezzo-Braren Studio
Illustrations: Loretta Trezzo Braren
Printing: Capital City Press

Williamson Publishing Co.
P.O. Box 185
Charlotte, Vermont 05445
1-800-234-8791

WILLIAMSON
KIDS CAN!

Manufactured in the United States of America

10 9 8 7 6 5 4 3 2 1

To Alex

CONTENTS

Acknowledgements

This book came about with the support and help of many people. I would like to thank all my students at The Saturday Academy for testing out the projects and giving input. Ben Ku was also a helpful advisor. Thanks to Kristina Beyer and Athena Papas at The Computer Store, and Michael Wingate, for their technical expertise and enthusiasm. Lori Clark planted the seed that got it all started. I am also indebted to Jack and Susan Williamson and Jennifer Ingersoll for their editorial expertise and personal warmth. And to my parents, Dave and Eileen Landstrom, two very creative people who have always encouraged me to use my imagination and to follow my dreams. Last, I would like to thank my husband, Alex Sabbeth, for his unending support and hard work in helping me with this book. He was involved at every stage of this dream.

READY, SET, ART!

People the world over have used their imaginations to create art since prehistoric times. And many times, as something new was discovered or invented, it changed the way they created. Using your computer to make something is a great way to be creative while having fun with your PC. It's exciting to turn an idea or a feeling into a masterpiece and even more satisfying knowing you made it yourself. Go as far as your imagination will take you — the sky's the limit!

A BRIEF HISTORY

Ancient peoples expressed their thoughts by drawing on the walls of caves with materials that were readily available. They made dyes from fruits and berries, and drawing tools from sticks and bones. Ancient Egyptians discovered that a reed could be soaked in water then made into a brush. This changed the style of their drawing and lettering. Up until the 1800s, artists were confined to their indoor studios, close to the materials they needed. But with the invention of collapsible tin tubes to hold paints, French Impressionists took to the beautiful outdoors. In fact, Claude Monet's garden and water lily paintings came about because of the invention of portable oil paints.

MONET WITH A MOUSE

Ahead are lots of great ideas for creating art and crafts — right on your computer! By using a computer as your drawing and painting tool, you can add new techniques to your art. The ability to copy, paste, and fill shapes with interesting patterns gives you endless ways to express yourself and have fun. Experiment with different layouts by dragging shapes around on the screen. You'll soon discover how easy it is to make changes as you work. Even creating personalized greeting cards requires a mere few clicks of a mouse!

Can I Shut Off My Computer Before Exiting?

It's tempting to shut your computer right off sometimes — especially when you're in a hurry — but don't do it! If you shut down without exiting the software program, you risk losing information and damaging the operating system (DOS or OS).

COMPUTERS, PRINTERS, SOFTWARE — AND CRAYONS, TOO!

There are many software programs that allow you to make art and crafts on your computer. Some paint and draw programs already exist on the software you have at home or school; many new computers come with painting software "bundled," or included, with the original purchase price. You can also buy a paint program of your own from the many good, inexpensive paint programs available.

You will need only two computer "tools" to make most of the projects: *a pencil or brush tool* that draws squiggly lines, and an eraser tool, because we all make mistakes — that's how we learn! An eraser tool icon, or symbol, may look like a stick of gum or the eraser on a pencil. The pencil or paintbrush tool usually looks like a squiggly line, a fat pencil,

PENCIL TOOL

or a paintbrush. Check out which programs your computer may already have for painting, and also check to see if your computer came with some paint programs that were never loaded. When you look on your hard disk, do you see any icons that look like drawing tools? If any of the programs have the word "Works" in them, take a look. When open, they should offer a drawing mode.

PAINTBRUSH TOOL

Along with your computer you will need a printer. For most projects, any printer will do. All activity instructions are written using black ink for printing; artwork is colored later with markers or crayons. If you have a color printer, you can add color right at the computer.

SMILEY KEYBOARD ART

One way to draw with your computer is by combining different keystrokes found on your keyboard. Add some fun to a typed message by adding a little face that expresses your words. These little faces are made up of colons, commas, parentheses, and other keystrokes. When put on their side, they look like a face. Here are a few smiley ideas. Can you think of more? Explore the keystrokes and special characters available on your software. Maybe you will discover other types of pictures. What would a smiley cat look like? Remember to turn them on their side when you look at them.

: -)	: - (	, •)	: - /
Smiley	Unhappy	Winky	Grouchy

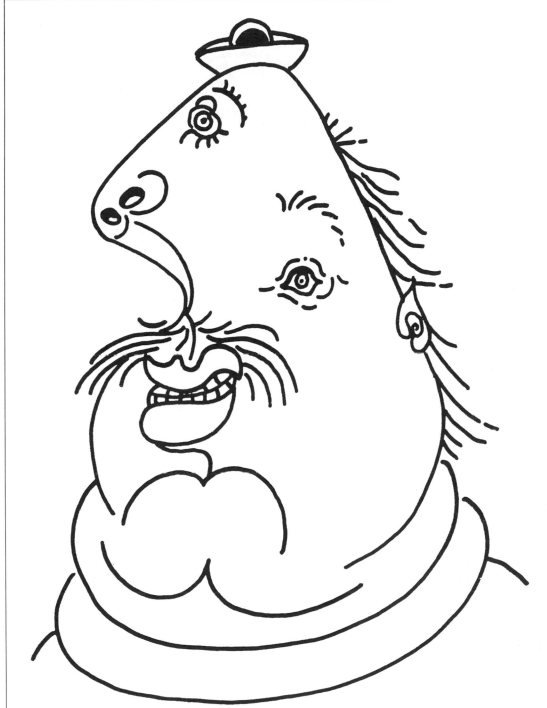

DIFFERENT STROKES

Of course, your drawings don't have to look at all like those used as examples in this book. That's where your artistry comes into play. How you draw should be an expression of who you are and how you feel. Every great artist has his or her own style. Maybe your style uses thin lines with delicate patterns. Or, perhaps you prefer bold, splashy strokes. Experiment with your tools to discover the combinations that work best for you.

Do what comes naturally; don't be concerned with how it is "supposed" to look. The only rule about making art is that there are no rules. We all have different ideas of what's fun, beautiful, or interesting. Browse through this book to see what meets your fancy. Add your personal creative flair! For instance, if you want to make a three-eyed goo-goo bug instead of a butterfly, go for it!

One famous artist of recent times, Pablo Picasso, could paint a "perfect" looking scene, exactly like the real thing — if he wanted to. But, he didn't want to. He could use a camera if he wanted it to look real! When asked why he didn't paint exact representations, he said, "I paint objects as I think them, not as I see them." So, if you "see" that the birthday cake you are drawing is small and still, but you "know" it tastes great and makes you excited about your birthday, then draw it big and bursting! Add confetti and streamers around it to express your excitement. If you keep Picasso's philosophy in mind, your art will not only be very imaginative, it will be truly your own!

GETTING STARTED

You will notice that each activity is identified by one mouse, two mice, or three mice. This is to give you an idea of the degree of difficulty involved in completing an activity, either at the computer or in the handwork. A "one-mouser" is less involved than a "three-mouser." You can jump in anywhere, but you might like to begin with some one-mousers to get started. Then go on to an activity that is a little more challenging. It's always a good idea to read all the instructions before starting.

After a while, you will start having your own ideas for computer creations. The first chapter, Mouse Doodles, is a great way to begin your adventure as a computer artist. There are six activities to get your creative juices flowing, while helping you get to know your paint program.

Are All Disks the Same?

If you have a tape recorder, you already know a little bit about computer disks. That's right, when you push Play or Record, your tape recorder uses a magnetic surface to play or record a song. A computer saves, accesses, and erases information on a magnetized disk, too. You've probably heard that computers have two types of disks — hard and floppy. So what's the difference between these two disks? Well, a *hard disk*, often called a *hard drive*, is a stiff aluminum disk built right into your computer. This aluminum disk has a special coating that allows information to be stored on it. Hard disks can store amazing amounts of information — many times the amount of a floppy disk.

Floppy disks, on the other hand, are inserted into your disk drive on the outside of your computer. Floppies are made of plastic film and covered with a magnetic coating. There are two types of floppy disks; *double density (DD)* and *high density (HD)*. Either type can work in most computers, but a HD disk holds more information than a DD disk. To remember this difference, think of HD as Heavy Duty.

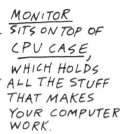

MONITOR SITS ON TOP OF CPU CASE, WHICH HOLDS ALL THE STUFF THAT MAKES YOUR COMPUTER WORK.

FLOPPY DISK DRIVE IS ON TOP OF THE HARD DRIVE, WHICH HOLDS A LOT OF INFO INCLUDING OPERATING SYSTEM AND SOFTWARE.

NEVER MOVE THIS SLIDING PIECE.

DISK LABEL SO YOU KNOW WHAT'S ON THIS DISK

DISK LOCK TAB
PUSH TAB ON OTHER SIDE OF DISK. SLIDE TAB SO HOLE IS COVERED TO CHANGE STUFF ON DISK. SLIDE TAB TO UNCOVER HOLE TO PROTECT DISK.

FLOPPY DISK

HELPFUL HINTS

It's pretty hard to break a computer, and usually if something goes wrong when you're working with a program, it's easily remedied. But, there are some things that could happen that wouldn't be so great.

✿ Don't drink or eat when working at your computer. Food and drink can get stuck in the keyboard or mouse and cause problems.

✿ When a project requires glue or paint, be sure to use these materials far away from your computer.

✿ Just as you put your toys neatly away, be sure you close all your programs and windows before shutting down your computer.

✿ Always keep your disks away from heat, direct sunlight, and magnets.

✿ Make a *folder* for yourself and keep all your work in it. Or, store your work on a floppy disk for safe keeping.

✿ If your computer is shared by the whole family, be careful of other people's documents. Don't delete any files that aren't your own.

TRACING TIP

Once in a while, you may love a drawing or pattern so much that you wish to draw something similar. To do this, place a piece of plastic wrap over the picture and trace it with a thin marker. Then, stick the piece of wrap on your computer monitor. Use the pencil tool on your computer to follow the traced lines of the wrap.

LET THE FUN BEGIN!

Remember, there are no rules when it comes to creating — just let your imagination run wild! Turn on your computer and get ready to discover the artist inside you!

MOUSE DOODLES

Think for a moment about how great musicians practice. They spend hours running up and down scales to loosen up. They sound terrific, but you won't recognize any songs as they practice. Similarly, these first activities are meant to "warm you up" without having any specific result in mind. By trying them out, you'll experience the freedom of being silly, spontaneous, and free-spirited in your art. But most of all, you'll have fun in the process!

MOUSE SURFING

All you need for this doodle activity is a sense of adventure! If you are new to using computers, ask a grown-up to help you with this activity and to scan the software's user guide with you.

WHAT YOU DO

1 Open your paint program.

2 Before you start drawing, take a good look at the *toolbox*. Can you figure out what all the little symbols, or *icons*, represent? Use your mouse to press and hold down on each tool. Do any extra menus pop up?

3 Scan or "surf" your menu bar by opening each menu and seeing what it has to offer. Do any words relate to drawing? Do you see words such as *Rotate*, *Group*, or *Flip*?

4 Okay, now you're ready to experiment! Pick up every tool in your toolbox one at a time, and see what it does. Just make crazy doodles; it doesn't matter what they look like!

5 Explore your menu commands. *Select* an item by *clicking* on it with a pointer tool. Some programs require *dragging* around the item with a special tool. Once you have selected an item, choose every command in the menu that sounds like a drawing function and watch what happens.

6 Print copies of your experimental art if you wish, and color.

What Is an Icon?

Icons are the little symbols you see on your screen when working in Windows® or on Macintosh® computers. Instead of typing a code to get into an application or document, you simply click on the symbol representing it. Icons usually look like what they can do. A painting program may have a paint-brush and palette as its icon. A writing program may look like a page of text. What do your icons look like?

SILLY SQUIGGLES

This will loosen up your way of thinking. Instead of thinking "I can't," say to yourself, "What if?"

WHAT YOU DO

1 Get silly! Think of a really ridiculous scene. Don't have too many details decided; it's better to just go with whatever pops up!

2 Start with a piece of clip art, scrapbook art, a number, shape, or just a quick squiggle on the screen. Add strokes, shapes, stamps, or patterns to make your silly scene. Use a lot of different tools to get used to what they can do. Try not to use your eraser too much. If something doesn't come out as you expected, change it into something else.

Pictures Made from Dots

If you were to look inside your monitor, or screen, you'd see thousands of tiny dots, or pixels, that light up and create an image on your screen. Believe it or not, each pixel is only $1/72$nd of an inch! Pixels have to be "told" by the computer to be "On" or "Off." If a pixel is on, it is lighted and looks white. If a pixel is off, it looks like a black dot.

MIXED MESSAGES

Learning computer lingo is a fun way to get hip with computers.
Here's a wacky way of looking at lingo while having some fun.

 **WHAT YOU DO**

1 What are some functions your computer can do? What are some computer terms you know? Forget what these words really mean and instead think of how they can be changed a little to have a whole new meaning.

2 Use your painting program to illustrate some mixed messages for these terms:

Computer Byte
_____

Megabyte
_____

Ink Jet
_____

CD-ROM
_____

Mouse Pad
_____

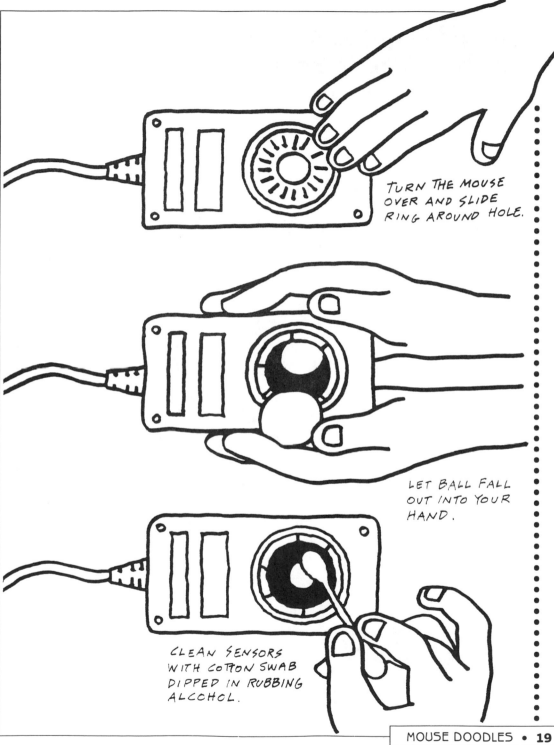

TURN THE MOUSE OVER AND SLIDE RING AROUND HOLE.

LET BALL FALL OUT INTO YOUR HAND.

CLEAN SENSORS WITH COTTON SWAB DIPPED IN RUBBING ALCOHOL.

Why Is a Mouse Called a Mouse?

Well, it is small, gray, and has a tail (sort of). Your cat may not be fooled, but if you stand back and squint your eyes, your computer mouse looks like a real rodent! To get the mouse to "talk" to the computer, you must press its button. Some fancy mice have several buttons that do things like automatically double click, cut, or paste. When you roll the mouse around its pad, a ball rolls inside the mouse and "tickles" its sensors, and its movement shows on your monitor.

Take a look inside: Hold your mouse upside down and look at its underside. With a grown-up's permission, slide the ring around the hole to release the small ball. Carefully turn the mouse over and let the ball fall out into your hand. Now take a look inside the mouse. Do you see the sensors? (Over time these sensors may get filled with lint. They can be cleaned with a cotton swab dipped in rubbing alcohol.) When you've finished looking, carefully put the ball back in and slide the collar into position. You won't want to do this too often because the ball could get lost. And without its ball, a mouse just won't work!

HORSE FEATHERS

Here's a great way to use your imagination! Start with a piece of clip art or draw your own subject to begin a bizarre journey.

WHAT YOU DO

1 Draw your own design, or place a piece of clip art on your screen. It can be an animal such as a horse, or a vegetable like a big squash, or any item really.

2 Go wild! Add your own touches to create a new type of creature. What would wings, feathers, or antlers look like on a horse? Why not draw a cow with stripes or a feathered pig? With your computer, you can make "the impossible" possible!

NEW, NEWER, NEWEST!

Computer Crime Stoppers

Computers do a lot of things for us, but did you ever think of them as keeping us all a little safer? Computers help police find criminals by keeping records about them on file so the police in any city can cross-check the files in another city.

Fingerprints, bullet fragments, blood samples, and fibers on clothing are analyzed quickly and accurately with the help of computers, too. In addition, various facial features are kept on computer to aid in identifying criminals. From the descriptions of a witness, police can select different examples of eyes, noses, and mouths to construct a picture of a suspect.

Funny face factory: On your computer, draw three different sets of eyes, noses, and mouths. Put these to one side of your screen. Next, draw an oval, or a head shape. Experiment with mixing and matching different features by dragging them onto the face. Add different hair styles. Make funny faces combining rabbit ears with a bird beak! Be outrageous!

COMPUTER Q&A

What's a "PC"?

Believe it or not, when computers were first invented, they often took up an entire room and were very expensive. Many people in large companies and work-places had to share these computers, called *main-frames*, by making a reservation to use it. Eventually technology allowed for smaller and cheaper computers, called *personal computers* or *PCs*, that could sit on a desk. This made it possible for anyone to have a PC.

Looking ahead: Personal computers keep getting smaller and more powerful. Just imagine what PCs might be like in the future! What might they look like and be able to do? Maybe you could wear one like a wristwatch! If you had a wish, what would you like your future computer to do for you?

MOUSE GONE WILD

Here's a fun "warm-up" game to play with a friend. Just let your mouse do the walking!

 **WHAT YOU DO**

1 Flip a coin to decide who will start the masterpiece. The first artist draws a simple shape or squiggle on the computer screen.

2 The second artist picks up where the first artist left off by adding a few strokes to the shape. Don't mention out loud what you think it will be. Let your friend decide what the next addition looks like. There's only one rule: You can't use the eraser tool! Every stroke is part of the masterpiece.

3 Take turns adding to the drawing, a few strokes at a time.

4 Continue taking turns until both artists decide the picture is finished. Were you both drawing the same thing?

5 You can also play this game alone, by drawing a squiggle and then seeing how many different things you can make it into.

Code Words

Computers are one of many tools people use to communicate. But did you know people were making letters into code long before today's computer codes were invented? The most famous coding system was created in the 1830s by Samuel Morse. That's right, the Morse Code! Mr. Morse gave each letter in the alphabet a combination of long and short taps, called dashes and dots. These taps were transmitted by telegraph wires that were strung across the country much like today's telephone lines. Telephones weren't invented yet, so people went to a telegraph office to send a message. Here's the code for the SOS call for help used around the world: ...－－－...

Getting the message: Type a Morse Code message to a friend, making dots with the period key (.) and dashes with the hyphen key (-). It's a lot of fun to communicate this way. Here's a message for you:

－－.－ －－－ －－－ ..

..－ －－－ .－.

－.－ －－ ...

Answer: Good for you

THE MORSE CODE SYSTEM

A .－	J .－－－	S ...
B －...	K －.－	T －
C －.－.	L .－..	U ..－
D －..	M －－	V ...－
E .	N －.	W .－－
F ..－.	O －－－	X －..－
G －－.	P .－－.	Y －.－－
H	Q －－.－	Z －－..
I ..	R .－.	

WACKY WORDS

Here's a way for you to turn words into art.

 **WHAT YOU DO**

1 Think of a word. Either type the word in very large letters in your paint program or draw the letters with tools from your toolbox.

2 Turn the word into what it means by adding art. Or, draw the word in a particular shape to illustrate its meaning.

3 Turn Wacky Words into a game. Put some fun words on separate pieces of paper into a container. Reach in and take a word; interpret the word through art. Then, someone else has a turn. If you are stumped about what to draw, then you're out.

DRAWING TIPS FROM YOUR TOOLBOX

There's lots to explore in your computer art toolbox (see pages 30–31).
Have fun trying out these awesome drawing techniques:

★ Use letters and symbols to draw a picture.

★ Make a cake with ovals and a few lines.

★ Make a 3-D square with the Copy/Paste function.

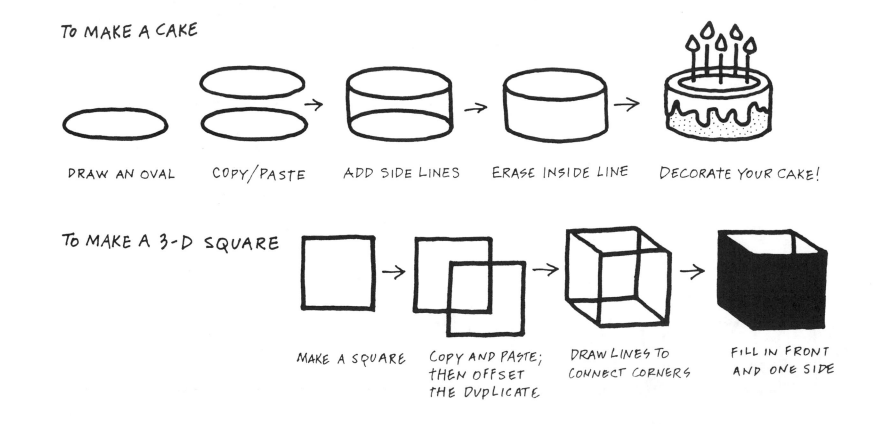

TO MAKE A CAKE

DRAW AN OVAL   COPY/PASTE   ADD SIDE LINES   ERASE INSIDE LINE   DECORATE YOUR CAKE!

TO MAKE A 3-D SQUARE

MAKE A SQUARE   COPY AND PASTE; THEN OFFSET THE DUPLICATE   DRAW LINES TO CONNECT CORNERS   FILL IN FRONT AND ONE SIDE

AROUND THE HOUSE

Nothing beats making something from scratch to use around the house! After all, creating something homemade can fill you with a real sense of accomplishment. And receiving something homemade is almost as gratifying, since your recipient will know that a lot of care and attention went into your gift.

E_DA_GERED SPECIES MAG_E_

Keep endangered species on the minds of everyone in your home with a refrigerator magnet collection of endangered animals. Make panda, African elephant, blue whale, and gorilla magnets to hold up important messages.

WHAT YOU NEED

Markers, several colors

Scissors

Glue stick

Small magnets

Poster board

 **WHAT YOU DO**

1 For each magnet, draw an endangered species like a panda. Then type a message such as "Save the Panda" below the picture. Draw a rectangle around the picture for a frame or make a fun border. Print 1 copy.

2 Cut out the picture, glue onto poster board, and color.

3 Glue a small refrigerator magnet or small piece of vinyl magnet to the back of the poster board.

SAVE THE PANDA

POSTER BOARD

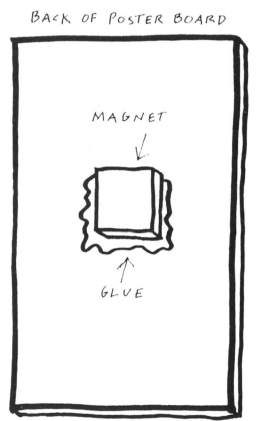

BACK OF POSTER BOARD

MAGNET

GLUE

WHAT'S IN YOUR TOOLBOX?

Some paint programs have tools and commands to help you arrange and move items. A great way to learn what your software can do is by experimenting. Draw a rectangle on the screen, then "select" it. (You know it is selected if it has small boxes surrounding it, or if it has a large dotted box, or *marquee*, surrounding it.) Try out different tools in your toolbox to see how they affect the selected rectangle. Can you make lots of rectangles by copying one over and over? Can you color in your rectangle making it a solid color? Can you draw a tree and place the rectangle in front of it or behind it?

Go to the menu bar and pull down each menu. Do any words look interesting? Try them out by choosing them, one at a time.

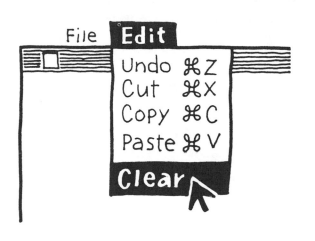

Here are some common icons to look for:

Icon	What it does	Icon	What it does
	Button with a shadow has a pop-up menu		Item can be rotated on the page
	Button with an arrow has a pop-up menu		Item can be flipped up/down and left/right
			Copy of item will be pasted on page
			Order of overlapping items will be switched
			Closed shape can be filled with colors or patterns

Here are some menu commands to look for:

Menu Command	What It Will Do
GROUP	Joins several items together to become one piece
SEND TO BACK	Places item behind items it currently covers
BRING TO FRONT	Places item in front of other items covering it
UNDO	Lets you undo your last step
FLIP	Will flip item horizontally or vertically
SHRINK/GROW	Will reduce or enlarge item selected
SHADOW	Creates a gray shadow of item selected

 # BEDROOM BLUEPRINT

Use your computer to help you create a whole new look in your bedroom! Working on screen makes it lots easier to experiment with different designs. After all, dragging your furniture across a screen sure beats dragging it across the room!

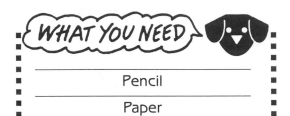

WHAT YOU NEED

Pencil

Paper

WHAT YOU DO

1 At your computer, draw a large rectangle representing your room. This is your *floor plan*. Add heavy lines to show windows and doors.

2 Outside the floor plan, draw the shapes of your furniture, imagining what each piece looks like from above. Keep each piece in proportion to the floor plan and to each other. For example, your computer should be smaller than your desk.

3 If possible, use the tool tips on page 31. Group elements that stay together. For instance, your computer monitor could be grouped with its keyboard and mouse to make it easier to move around within your floor plan.

4 Does your software allow you to rotate or flip your drawings? If not, draw the same piece at various angles.

5 Drag the pieces around the floor plan to come up with a plan you like. Print out as many different plans as you wish.

6 Now that you've used your brains, it's time to use your brawn, by trying out your plan!

Hint: Offer to help design someone's room in exchange for help moving your furniture.

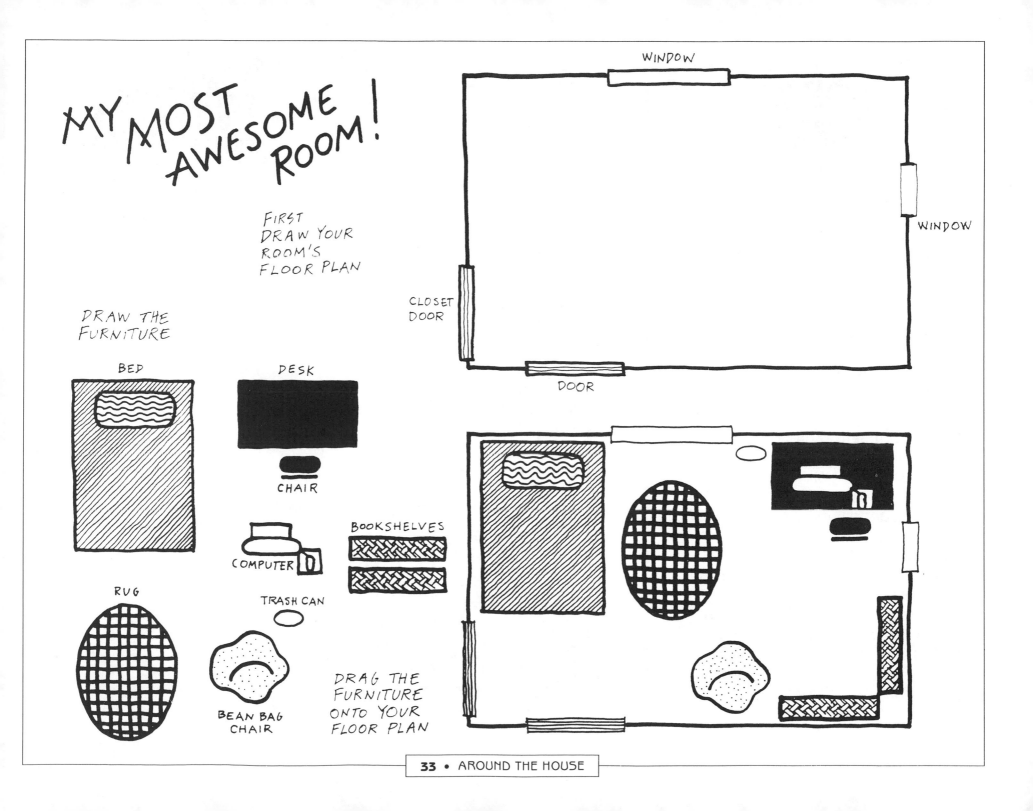

MY MOST AWESOME ROOM!

FIRST DRAW YOUR ROOM'S FLOOR PLAN

WINDOW

WINDOW

CLOSET DOOR

DOOR

DRAW THE FURNITURE

BED

DESK

CHAIR

COMPUTER

BOOKSHELVES

RUG

TRASH CAN

BEAN BAG CHAIR

DRAG THE FURNITURE ONTO YOUR FLOOR PLAN

What Is a Bit?

Contrary to what most people believe, computers aren't all that smart. After all, they can only count from zero to one! In fact, they only "know" if a particular circuit is ON or OFF. Computers count OFF as "0" and ON as "1." These tiny bits of information are called just that, *bits*. A bit, short for *Binary digit*, is the smallest unit of information a computer works with.

See for yourself: Pretend you are a circuit in a computer. Go to a light switch and turn it on; now you have current. Your bit would be a "1." Now turn the light off and your bit would be a "0." Turn the switch on and off a few times. This is just what your computer is doing when it processes information. Of course it goes much, much faster than you or I could move the switch. Just think, in order to be as fast as today's computers, you would have to be able to move the switch millions of times in one second!

Computing With Beads

The great, great grandfather of today's computer, the *abacus*, was created about 5,000 years ago and is still used today. An abacus consists of rows of beads strung on a series of wires with each bead representing a number. Numbers are added together by moving the beads. Your school or local library may even have an abacus you could try out.

Does Your Font Have Feet?

What a question you say! Have you ever noticed that some of the type styles, or *fonts*, on your computer have feet and others do not? The first people to add *serifs*, or feet to their letters were the ancient Romans. Back then, messages were written by chiseling them into stone tablets. It was easier (and also neater) if they first chiseled the feet of the letter, then used a bigger chisel to cut the letter's main shape. Today, people believe "feet" or serif type styles, help us read a long line of type, such as in a storybook. So next time you read a book and see letters with "feet," think of them as helping you "walk" through the words!

 # FLOWER POT HERB GARDEN

Make little signs to identify herbs you grow inside. Try thyme, rosemary, and basil. Decorate each pot with a butterfly or ladybug design. Then, cook up your harvest in an omelette!

WHAT YOU NEED

- Colored printer paper
- Construction paper
- Scissors
- Glue stick
- Assorted herbs
- Pots and soil
- Toothpicks, tape

 ## WHAT YOU DO

1 Draw a 3" × 2" (7.5 cm × 5 cm) rectangle. Type the name of an herb you plan to grow inside the shape. Decorate with borders, leaves, or pretty designs.

2 Repeat for other herbs.

Hint: Copy the first rectangle and paste duplicates to keep sizes the same.

3 Print on colored paper. Cut out and glue shapes onto construction paper. Cut out, leaving a 1/2" (1 cm) border around your artwork. Tape each sign onto a toothpick.

4 Plant your garden. Fill pots with soil. Plant seeds of one type in each pot, and water. Place sign in proper pot in a sunny window, and watch your garden grow!

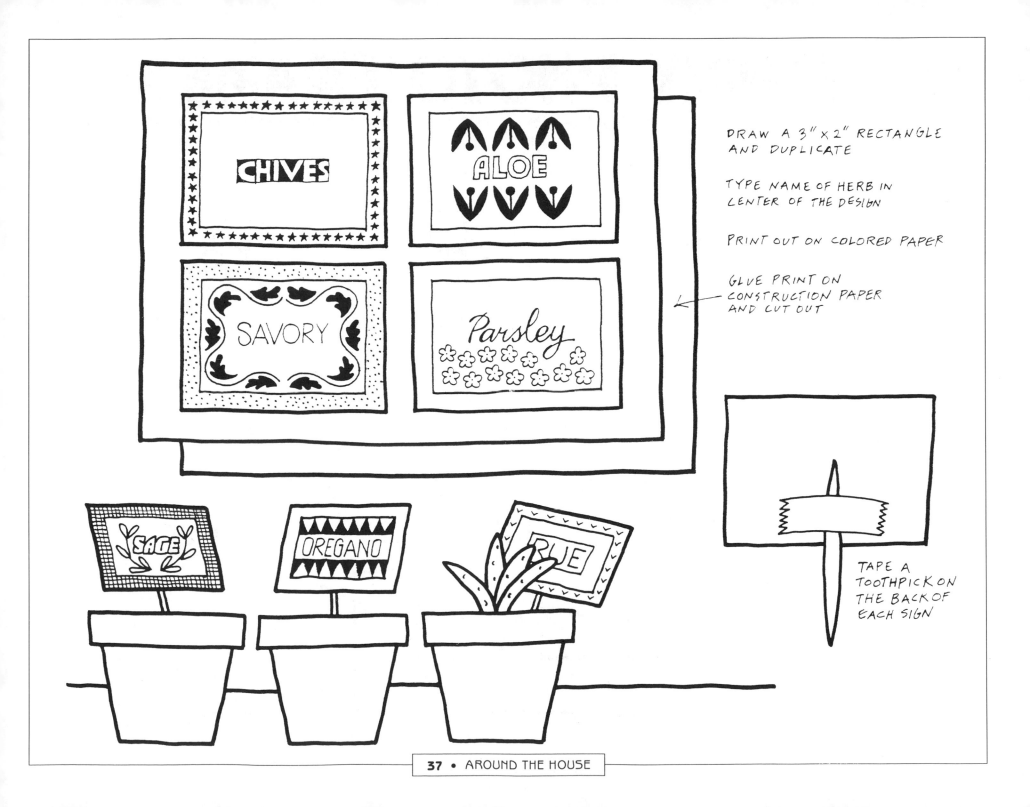

DRAW A 3" x 2" RECTANGLE AND DUPLICATE

TYPE NAME OF HERB IN CENTER OF THE DESIGN

PRINT OUT ON COLORED PAPER

GLUE PRINT ON CONSTRUCTION PAPER AND CUT OUT

TAPE A TOOTHPICK ON THE BACK OF EACH SIGN

FUNKY PHOTO FRAME

Homemade photo frames are much more special than store-bought. Create different border designs and glue on a small magnet to display on your refrigerator.

WHAT YOU NEED

Scissors

Poster board

Markers, several colors

Glue stick

1 Measure a picture that you want to frame.

2 Draw a rectangle on your screen, a little smaller than your picture. Draw another rectangle, about 1/2" (1 cm) larger, around the first, creating a border or frame.

3 Decorate the frame with funky designs. Print a copy and cut out along the outside line. Color your frame any way you wish. Cut out center where the picture will go, along the inner rectangle.

4 Cut another rectangle from poster board for a backing sheet, and set aside. To mount, glue the frame to the photo. Then glue the backing sheet to the picture back.

5 To make a stand, cut a piece of poster board in a wide strip about 3/4 of the height of the picture. Bend the strip's top over, position so bottom of strip will touch tabletop, and glue bent portion to picture backing.

MEASURE PICTURE

I · ♡ GRANDMA

CUT OUT CENTER OF FRAME

I · ♡ GRANDMA

GLUE FRAME TO PICTURE TO BACKING

GLUE TO BACKING

FOLD

STAND

Connecting Our World

If you want to link your computer with computers across town or around the world, all you need is a piece of hardware called a *modem*. A modem uses normal telephone lines to connect your PC to outside computers. Many modern computers come with modems already installed inside them. Or, you can buy a separate, external modem that hooks up to the back of your computer.

If you want to get on the Internet (see page 154), the on-line service you choose will provide special software to get your modem hooked up. Internet users pay a monthly fee for on-line services. But you don't need an on-line service if you want to send messages back and forth to a friend who also has a modem. The communications software needed may be on your computer already.

A MAN OF MANY STYLES

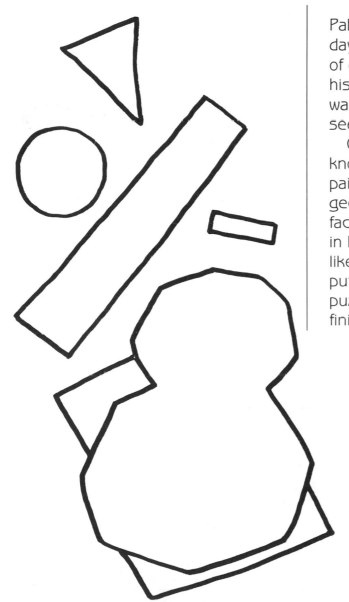

Pablo Picasso spent nearly every day of his 93-year life creating art of one kind or another. He used his creativity to surprise people; to wake them up to a new way of seeing the world.

One of his painting styles was known as *Cubism*. It turned his paintings into a composition of geometric shapes on a flat surface. Picasso constructed images in his paintings using what looked like small painted cubes that he put together one at a time, like a puzzle, until the entire picture was finished.

CUBIST COASTERS

Create some coasters in the style Picasso loved — Cubism! It's a fun way to experiment with shapes. And because your computer lets you save the original and use "Save As" for variations, it is easy to come up with many ideas.

WHAT YOU NEED

Glue

Markers, several colors

Cardboard

Scissors

Varnish

 **WHAT YOU DO**

1 Draw several shapes on your screen, such as ovals, rectangles, polygons. Save file and title it "Shapes."

2 Create a coaster design by going to the *File menu* and choosing *Save As*. Name the file "Coaster 1."

3 Click onto a shape and drag it to make new pictures. Add small details if you wish, such as eyes, a tail, or feathers. When complete, make sure your changes are saved. Print 1 copy.

4 Open the file titled "Shapes" and repeat the process. Make a different creation using the same shapes. Print 1 copy.

5 Continue opening the original "Shapes" file, creating and printing new images.

6 Add color to each piece of art, then glue to a square or circle of cardboard. Cut out.

7 Varnish each coaster to make waterproof and shiny. Let dry.

DRAW SEVERAL SHAPES ON YOUR SCREEN

DUPLICATE A SHAPE

DRAW A DESIGN INSIDE A SHAPE

COLOR DESIGNS ON PRINT

GLUE PRINTOUT ON CARDBOARD, CUT OUT COASTERS.

GLUE

CARDBOARD

JAM JAR LABELS

Canning fruits, vegetables, or jam is a great way to preserve the summer season. And making homemade jar labels adds a personal touch you can enjoy year-round!

WHAT YOU NEED

- Scissors
- Markers, several colors
- Glue stick
- Ribbon
- Fabric scraps
- Glass jars with lids
- Jam (see recipe, page 46)

MY PICKLES

STRAWBERRY Jam

GROUP AND COPY LABEL ART. PASTE LABELS TO FIT ON PAGE. PRINT OUT AND COLOR.

1 On your computer, draw a big rectangular label.

2 Give your jam company a name and design an eye-catching logo for the label. Add a few berries or other fruit shapes to your design.

3 Print as many copies as you have jars. Color labels and set aside.

4 Make jam (see page 46). Wipe jars clean, and glue on labels.

5 Cut a circle of fabric, larger than the jar's lid. Lay fabric on top of jam lid, and tie jar neck with ribbon.

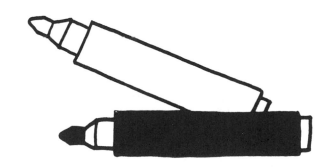

ERIC'S EASY STRAWBERRY JAM

This jam recipe is easy to make, since there's no need to add paraffin.
Just store this jam in the refrigerator for a delicious treat. Yields 5 cups.

WHAT YOU NEED

2 cups (500 ml) strawberries,
hulled and washed

4 cups (1 l) sugar

3/4 cup (175 ml) water

2 tablespoons (25 ml)
fruit pectin

1 tablespoon (15 ml)
lemon juice

Saucepan

Large wooden spoon

DON'T FORGET TO REMOVE THE STEMS

PUT BERRIES IN A BOWL AND CRUSH WITH FORK

WHAT YOU DO

1 Put strawberries in a large bowl, and crush them with a fork. Pour sugar over the berries and let mixture sit about 15 minutes.

2 Ask a grown-up to help you boil the water in a small saucepan. Add the pectin and continue boiling for about 2 minutes or until the pectin is dissolved. Stir.

3 Pour water-pectin mixture over the strawberries, and crush the berries a little more while stirring the mixture. Mix in the lemon juice.

4 Pour the jam into glass jars that have been sterilized (with grown-up help) for 10 minutes in boiling water. Fill the jars only about 2/3 full. Put on lids according to package directions, and cool overnight at room temperature.

5 Put jam in the refrigerator. Be sure to give a few jars to some neighbors for a special treat.

USE STERILIZED JARS

FILL JARS 2/3 FULL

Do All Letters Have Feet?

Letters without feet are called *sans serif*, which is French for "without stroke." About fifty years ago, a group of designers thought type would look more modern if it were less fancy, so they developed sans serif letters that looked clean and crisp. Sans serif is easy to read when only a few words are used in a large size. Just take a look at a STOP sign. It's easy to read, isn't it? That's because STOP signs, and lots of others, too, are often written in a sans serif font.

One of the most popular footless fonts used is named *Helvetica*, a word derived from the Latin name for Switzerland, *Helvetia*. And as you may have already guessed, Helvetica was designed during the 1950s in — you guessed it — Switzerland.

Experiment with fonts: Open any software program on your computer that lets you type letters. How many fonts does your computer have? Go to the menu named "Type" or "Font." If it has ten font choices, type your name ten times in a large point size (6 point is very small; type gets bigger as numbers get higher). Then, make your name in a different font each time. Notice those fonts with feet and those without. Print and keep on hand to glance at when choosing a font.

INK-JET PRINTER:

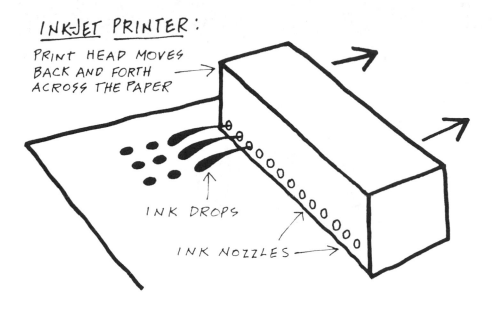

PRINT HEAD MOVES BACK AND FORTH ACROSS THE PAPER

INK DROPS

INK NOZZLES

LASER PRINTER:

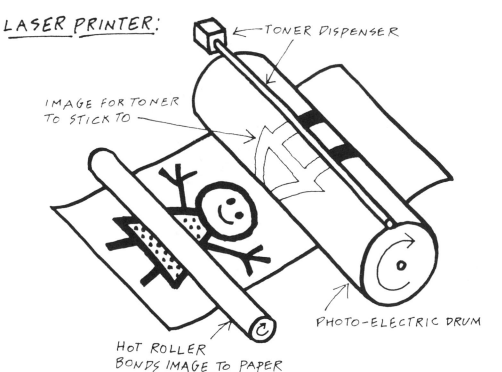

TONER DISPENSER

IMAGE FOR TONER TO STICK TO

HOT ROLLER BONDS IMAGE TO PAPER

PHOTO-ELECTRIC DRUM

Printer Picks

You already know computers come in many styles and with different capabilities, but did you know printers do, too? Printers come in three main types:

The *dot-matrix* printer uses a printing head that contains up to 24 tiny wires. Each wire is pressed against the inked ribbon by electrical signals in the printer, producing dots on the page that form letters, numbers, and other characters.

Ink-jet printers spray tiny droplets of ink on the page. Amazingly, the resulting characters are virtually as sharp as those from a laser printer. Ink-jet printers are the most common printers used to produce color.

Laser printers use a miniature laser beam and black powder called "toner" to print characters. They are the fastest and clearest of printers, and can print in color, too.

BUTTERFLY NOTE HOLDER

Use note holders for place cards at the dinner table or to hold a grocery list or phone message. Make a monarch or viceroy design, or let your own idea take flight!

BUTTERFLY NOTE HOLDER

WHAT YOU NEED

- Wooden spring-type clothespin
- Garbage bag twist tie
- Scissors
- Markers, several colors
- Glue stick
- Construction paper

 **WHAT YOU DO**

1 Draw a rectangle the size of a clothespin in the center of the screen. You may wish to hold a clothespin to the screen and trace it with the mouse. This is your butterfly body.

2 On each side of the body, draw and decorate a large wing. Print out and color as you wish.

3 Glue the undecorated side of the butterfly to construction paper. Cut out.

4 To assemble the butterfly, glue the undecorated side of the body to a clothespin. Fold the wings up. Glue a folded twist tie at top of closed end for antennae.

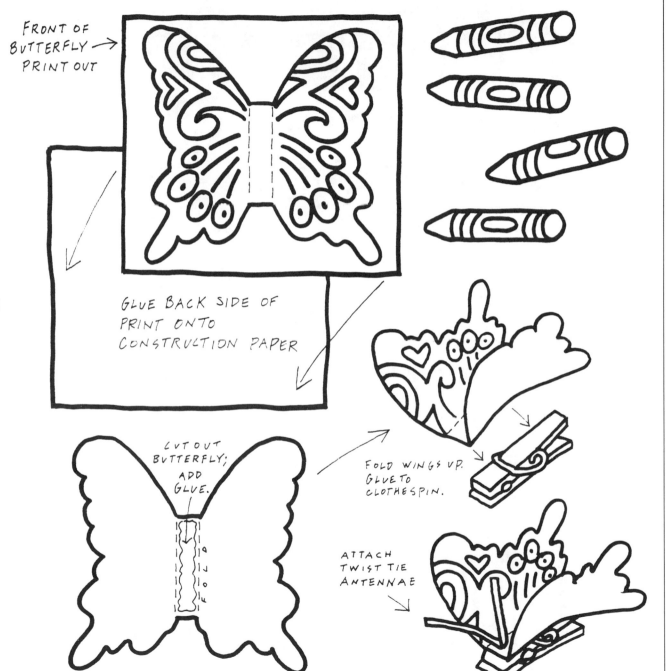

FRONT OF BUTTERFLY PRINT OUT

GLUE BACK SIDE OF PRINT ONTO CONSTRUCTION PAPER

CUT OUT BUTTERFLY; ADD GLUE.

FOLD WINGS UP. GLUE TO CLOTHESPIN.

ATTACH TWIST TIE ANTENNAE

What Is a Byte?

Just as one word from a book tells you very little about a story, one bit (see page 34) doesn't tell a computer much of anything either. That's why computers string many zeros and ones together into a message. When eight bits are strung together, they make a byte, something software designers use as their basic building block. The byte for just the letter A reads: 01000001. Imagine the bytes it would take to write a whole book!

Making bytes into words: Here are the bytes for the letters A, T, and C. How many word combos can you make from these letters? Try writing out the letters' bytes in the correct order to make a word. For a real challenge, take turns with a friend "decoding" a simple message or two.

A = 01000001

T = 01010100

C = 01000011

CLEVER CRAFTS

Computer creativity can be purely practical, as in making noteholders, and it can also be purely fun as in making greeting cards. One goal that computer artists share with all creative people is devising clever ways to recycle materials in our efforts to save the Earth. That's why you will find here Floppy Art based on recycling floppy disks and lots of ideas for putting old computer printouts to creative use.

FLOPPY ART

Wait! Don't throw out those old disks — recycled floppies make terrific bookmarks, jewelry, and wind chimes!

WHAT YOU NEED

3 old 3.5" (8.5 cm) floppy disks
Glue stick
Puffy fabric paint
Markers, several colors
1 old post-style earring
String
Scissors

WHAT YOU DO

First, dissect a disk as explained on page 55, saving all three parts.

For Bookmarks:

The floppy's hard case makes a great bookmark. Just slide it over a page to mark your place. Or, make a giant paper clip to hold your art work together. Use your computer to design new labels. Then cut out, color, and glue onto the case.

For Floppy Jewelry:

The inside disk makes a fun piece of jewelry. Cut designs in the plastic and decorate with fabric paint. Attach your design as you would a pin to a shirt or jacket with an old post earring. Push the post through the floppy's center hole, then through the piece of clothing. Close the back with the earring's clasp.

PLACE EARRING POST THROUGH THE HOLE

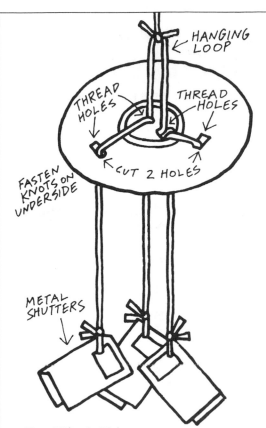

HANGING LOOP

THREAD HOLES

THREAD HOLES

FASTEN KNOTS ON UNDERSIDE

CUT 2 HOLES

METAL SHUTTERS

For Wind Chimes:

Make a high-tech wind chime from 3 recycled disks. Cut 3 pieces of string to 10" (25 cm) lengths and attach one piece to each metal shutter. Cut 2 small holes in one floppy's inside plastic ring (save the other two rings for another project). Thread string through the holes and tie. Hang the metal shutters so that they will tap one another when the wind blows. Hang the disk with a loop of string in a breezy spot.

COMPUTER Q&A

Why Aren't Floppy Disks Floppy?

SLIP OFF SHUTTER

PRY OPEN HARD CASE

SLIDE DISK OUT

At first glance a floppy disk doesn't look very floppy, does it? But look again. Inside its hard plastic outer case that protects from dirt and dust, a floppy disk has a small circular ring of thin plastic that is floppy. This is where messages are stored. But one thing a hard case can't protect a disk from is a magnet. Magnets will destroy the information on a disk, so be careful!

Dissect-a-disk: Let's operate! A floppy disk can be used again and again, but if you have a damaged one, dissect it. You'll find three parts: a metal shutter, a hard outer case, and an inside floppy plastic ring. Slide the metal shutter back and forth and carefully slip the shutter away from the hard case. Next, ask a grown-up to help you pry open the exposed edge of the case with a dull butter knife. Once open, slide out the dark piece of plastic — the floppy. It doesn't look like much, but it is covered with a magnetic film that stores your typed information as zeros and ones (see page 34).

VINCENT'S SEED PACKETS

Begin with a Vincent van Gogh-inspired design, then create a series of seed packets based on other famous artists. Choose Georgia O'Keeffe for poppies, or Claude Monet for wildflowers. Include a brief saying about the artist next to the planting instructions.

WHAT YOU NEED

Glue stick

Scissors

Markers, several colors

Sunflower seeds

SEED PACKET FRONT FACES OUT

VINCENT'S
SUNFLOWERS

APPLY GLUE STICK TO BLANK SIDE OF SEED PACKET.

DO NOT GLUE TOP.

SEED PACKET BACK (BLANK SIDE)

FILL PACKET WITH SUNFLOWER SEEDS AND GLUE TOP OF PACKET

VINCENT'S
SUNFLOWERS

 **WHAT YOU DO**

1 Draw a 3" x 4" (7.5 cm x 10 cm) rectangle. Copy and paste a second rectangle next to the first. These are the front and back of your seed packet.

2 Design the packet front with sunflowers (for a van Gogh-inspired packet), imaginative decorations, and the name of your seed company.

3 On the back, type planting instructions and a brief remark about Vincent van Gogh, the Dutch artist renowned for his sunflower paintings.

4 Print 1 copy for each packet. Color and cut out. Glue fronts to backs along the edges, leaving the top open.

5 Fill with sunflower seeds, and glue the top shut. Or, cover with clear contact paper, and mount on sticks to use as row markers.

THEN & NOW

Saving Lives

Medical science has been revolutionized by computers. In hospitals, some machines help damaged organs function properly. Dialysis machines filter and clean blood. Inside the body, a person's weak heart can be strengthened by a computer called a "pace-maker."

Today, doctors can even look inside the body without performing surgery. Ultrasound machines allow doctors to view organs using sound waves. Images are seen on a screen or monitor after they are converted from sound, using computer technology. Patients can see images of their own heart beating, and a mom-to-be can see the beating heart of her unborn baby!

 # CHICKADEE CAFE

Bring the birds in your neighborhood right to your window with a birdseed cafe. Make a feeder for larger birds out of a gallon milk carton and call it the Rockin' Robin Diner!

WHAT YOU NEED

Pint-sized milk carton

Glue stick, scissors

Markers, several colors

Stick or pencil

Toothpick

Hole punch

Yarn

Birdseed

 ## WHAT YOU DO

1 To make side panels of cafe, draw a rectangle the size of a face of the milk carton. Decorate with a window and flower box. Print 2 copies and cut out.

2 Draw another rectangle for the cafe's roof panels. It should be about the size of the sloped top of the carton. Draw a sign that says "CHICKADEE CAFE" and another saying "EAT!" Print 2 copies of each drawing and cut out.

3 Cut out two opposite sides of milk carton, leaving 1" (2.5 cm) at bottom for a lip. Punch a hole in center of lip on each side. Insert a stick through holes for a bird perch.

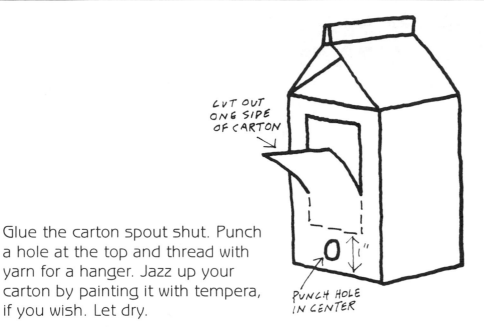

CUT OUT
ONE SIDE
OF CARTON

PUNCH HOLE
IN CENTER

1"

4 Glue the carton spout shut. Punch a hole at the top and thread with yarn for a hanger. Jazz up your carton by painting it with tempera, if you wish. Let dry.

5 Color side and roof panels, and glue each to the carton side and top. Glue the two "EAT" signs together, back-to-back with a toothpick sandwiched between. Poke toothpick into roof.

6 Fill feeder with birdseed and hang outside near a window. Watch for feathered customers!

SIGN
PRINT 2, CUT OUT
AND GLUE TOOTHPICK
BETWEEN FRONT
AND BACK PANELS.
INSERT SIGN IN
THE ROOF.

EAT

CHICKADEE
CAFE

ROOF
PRINT 2, CUT
OUT, AND GLUE
TO TOP OF CARTON.

SIDE PANELS
PRINT 2, CUTOUT;
THEN GLUE TO
LOWER SIDES
OF CARTON

INSERT STICK
OR PENCIL IN
HOLE FOR
BIRD PERCH

Doing Chores

All computers come with a software program or operating system that allows them to do their basic chores. One chore your computer does is organize and manage files you create. The operating system used on IBM PCs and clones is the Disk Operating System, or DOS for short. Apple® Computer also makes a PC, called a Macintosh®, that uses a different operating system than DOS, called simply OS.

 # MOUSE HOUSE

Make a cute mouse cover to protect your mouse from dust — and keep you company while you work. Create other "mouse house" figures such as a dog, an elephant, or a big wedge of Swiss cheese!

 **WHAT YOU NEED**

Glue stick

Stapler

Scissors

Paper, pink and gray

2 pink pipe cleaners

 **WHAT YOU DO**

1 Draw an outline of a mouse, about twice the size of your computer mouse. Draw eyes and print 2 copies on gray paper.

2 Draw ears and a nose. Print 1 copy on pink paper.

3 Cut pieces out. Place the 2 mouse bodies on top of each other, so that eyes show on one side only. Staple around the outside, leaving back end open.

4 Staple two pipe cleaners for whiskers. Glue nose over pipe cleaners. Glue on ears. Place your mouse in its new home.

1. DRAW SHAPE TWICE THE SIZE OF YOUR MOUSE.

2. DRAW EARS & NOSE. PRINT OUT ON PINK PAPER.

3. CUT OUT ALL PRINTED PIECES. STAPLE BODY PIECES TOGETHER, PRINTED SIDES UP!

4. STAPLE ON PIPE CLEANERS. GLUE ON NOSE & EARS.

5. PUT THE MOUSE INTO THE HOUSE.

NEW, NEWER, NEWEST!

Doodling Devices

Drawing with a mouse might seem a lot like drawing with a bar of soap! But with a little practice, it's not too hard to control a mouse. Apple® was the first company to use a mouse with its PCs. They discovered that a mouse made using a computer easy. Still, wouldn't it be nice to draw with a pen on screen? Many professional illustrators think so, too. In fact, most now use a *graphics tablet*, a pen-like device that presses down on a special mouse pad.

FINGERPRINT STATIONERY

Here's some one-of-a-kind stationery made with your one and only fingerprint!
Think of how many pictures you can make with fingerprints. How about birds
perched in a tree? Or, use a turkey design for a Thanksgiving note.

WHAT YOU NEED

6" x 4" (15 cm x 10 cm)
envelope

Color ink pad

Scissors

Colored paper, 8½" x 11"
(21 cm x 27.5 cm)

Scrap paper

Glue stick

THIS LITTLE MOUSE SAYS "COME TO MY HOUSE!"

HI

I MISS YOU

1 Cut the colored paper to fit the envelope when folded.

2 On your computer, draw a rectangle about 1" smaller (both width and height) than the envelope. Type a special message such as "A Special Note from Jamie to YOU!" Decorate the page with stars or cars or a special border. (See clip art, page 93.)

ENVELOPE

FOLD IN HALF

You're One of a Kind!

GLUE PRINT ONTO COLORED PAPER

3 Print and cut out. Glue designed page onto outside of folded colored paper. Press your finger onto the ink pad; then press firmly onto card. Draw details around fingerprints to create a picture.

PRESS FINGER INTO INK PAD; THEN ONTO CARD.

NEW, NEWER, NEWEST!

Good News for Old Computers

Does your old computer lack the memory and speed of newer models? Don't despair! Most older computers can be *upgraded* for more speed, memory, or other capabilities. For instance, some 286 chip computers can be upgraded in several ways. Modifications can be made to many older computers so they can run today's more advanced color monitors, too.

If you really do need a newer model computer, be sure to place your old computer in a new home. Many people only use the word processing capabilities, and an older model is perfect for their needs!

POP-UP GREETING CARD

In a pinch for a special greeting card? Here's a card you can use for any occasion! Send different messages to different people by making several variations of the same card.

WHAT YOU NEED

Colored printer paper

Glue stick

Scissors

Markers, several colors

Mother

Day: _____

Time: _____

Dad

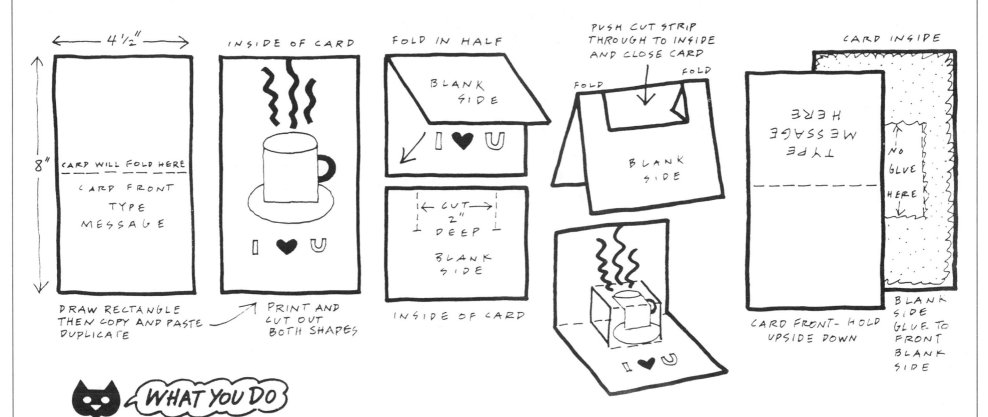

Labels within the illustration (top row, left to right):

4 1/2"

8"

CARD WILL FOLD HERE

CARD FRONT
TYPE
MESSAGE

DRAW RECTANGLE
THEN COPY AND PASTE
DUPLICATE

INSIDE OF CARD

I ♥ U

PRINT AND
CUT OUT
BOTH SHAPES

FOLD IN HALF

BLANK SIDE

I ♥ U

← CUT →
2"
DEEP
BLANK SIDE

INSIDE OF CARD

PUSH CUT STRIP
THROUGH TO INSIDE
AND CLOSE CARD

FOLD   FOLD

BLANK SIDE

I ♥ U

CARD INSIDE

TYPE
MESSAGE
HERE

NO GLUE HERE

CARD FRONT- HOLD
UPSIDE DOWN

BLANK SIDE GLUE TO FRONT BLANK SIDE

🐱 **WHAT YOU DO**

1 Draw a 4.5" x 8" (11 cm x 20 cm) rectangle. Copy and paste a duplicate next to it.

2 To make the outside of the card, type your message in the bottom half of one rectangle.

3 Design the card's inside by making a picture that falls in the center of the other rectangle.

4 Add a message at the bottom of the rectangle.

5 Print 1 copy. Cut out the 2 large rectangle shapes to make the cover and inside of your card.

6 Fold the picture rectangle in half, top to bottom so the picture does not show. Make cuts on each side of the drawing, about 2" (5 cm) long. Push the cut strip through to the other side of the card. Close the card and open to test the pop-up section.

7 Glue rectangle everywhere but behind the cut-out. Glue rectangles, with one card flipped up, back to back. Fold card so that the inside art folds out when the card is closed.

RECYCLE YOUR COMPUTER PRINTOUTS

Recycling is a great way to preserve our natural resources and save our environment from pollution. And, recycling just plain feels good, too! Offices that use a lot of paper often recycle it. They separate the white and colored paper, and send it to a recycling plant where it's turned into paper products we can use again. Here are a few ways you can recycle printed paper, too!

PAPER DOLLS

PAPER FLOWERS

MASKS

HOLIDAY DECORATIONS

Once paper is printed on one side, reinsert it for printing on the clean side. Determine the side your printer prints on by drawing an arrow, pointing up, on one side of a piece of paper. Put the page into the printer drawer, face up with the arrow pointing away from you. Type a message on your computer and print one page. Did the computer message fall on the side with the arrow? If so, it prints on the top of the paper.

Put a large box under your printer. After paper has been used up, toss in the box. When the box is full, bring it to a recycling center.

Think of creative uses for used printer paper, such as a papier-mache craft. Spread used paper on the table when working on a messy project, or crunch it into balls and use for packing when mailing a package.

Make high-tech gift wrap and tie package with twine, or sponge paint for pretty gift wrap. Use a hole punch to make paper doilies or confetti.

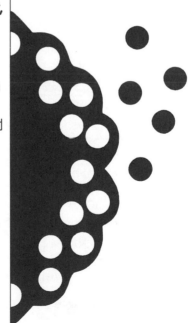

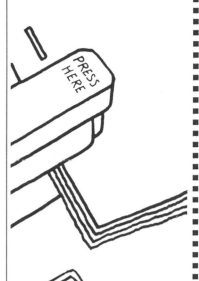

Gather used sheets of different colors and clip together or sew together with yarn for scrap note paper for messages.

Flight of Fancy

When the Wright brothers invented the first airplane, they used only a few simple parts to fly their contraption. Today, pilots rely on computers to help them navigate. Computers can even help planes use fuel efficiently and keep track of the location of other planes in the sky. Have you ever heard a flight attendant ask passengers to avoid using electronic devices such as radios, cellular phones, and remote-controlled toys? This is because those devices emit radio waves that interfere with the plane's computerized navigational systems.

Airlines also use computers on the ground to make reservations for millions of customers. Computers keep track of each seat on a plane, so when you make a reservation, your seat number will be assigned to you and to no one else.

ART FOR ART'S SAKE

Think of your computer as another wonderful tool in your art supply box. Instead of picking up your paintbrush, click on your mouse to create beautiful designs. Combining your computer with traditional artists' materials such as construction paper, markers, and paint will produce dramatic results. And making multiple copies of your works of art is easy — just change the number of printouts you make! Before long, you'll discover that using your computer as a painter's palette is a great way to express your creativity.

"STAINED-GLASS" LIGHT CATCHER

Catch the sun each day in your "stained-glass" window!

WHAT YOU NEED

Scissors

Tape

Markers, several colors

Plastic wrap

 **WHAT YOU DO**

1 Draw a picture, using big bold sections that can be cut out.

2 Print the picture, then carefully cut out big sections, such as the petals of a flower.

3 Tape plastic wrap (carefully smoothed out) on back of paper so wrap shows through the cut-out design.

FRONT OF PRINT

CUT OUT
LARGE SECTIONS
OF PRINT

TAPE PLASTIC
WRAP ON BACK
OF PRINT AND
COLOR THE
SECTIONS

4 With plastic wrap face up, color each section with brightly colored markers. Let dry. Add fine details and outline shapes in black, if you wish.

5 Put your light catcher in a window, with the wrap to the glass. Watch the colors light up when the sun shines through!

Who Invented the Microchip?

The first *microprocessor*, also known as a microchip, was developed by Intel Corporation in 1970. It incorporated a few thousand transistors into a tiny sliver of silicon and could perform about 50,000 operations per second! Intel is the same company that invented the Pentium® chip, capable of performing *millions* of operations in a single second!

FALLING STAR

Hang these in a window or place on gifts as bows. Or, draw balloons on your star and type "HAPPY BIRTHDAY!" several times for party favors.

WHAT YOU NEED

Glue stick

Scissors

Colored printer paper

Ribbon

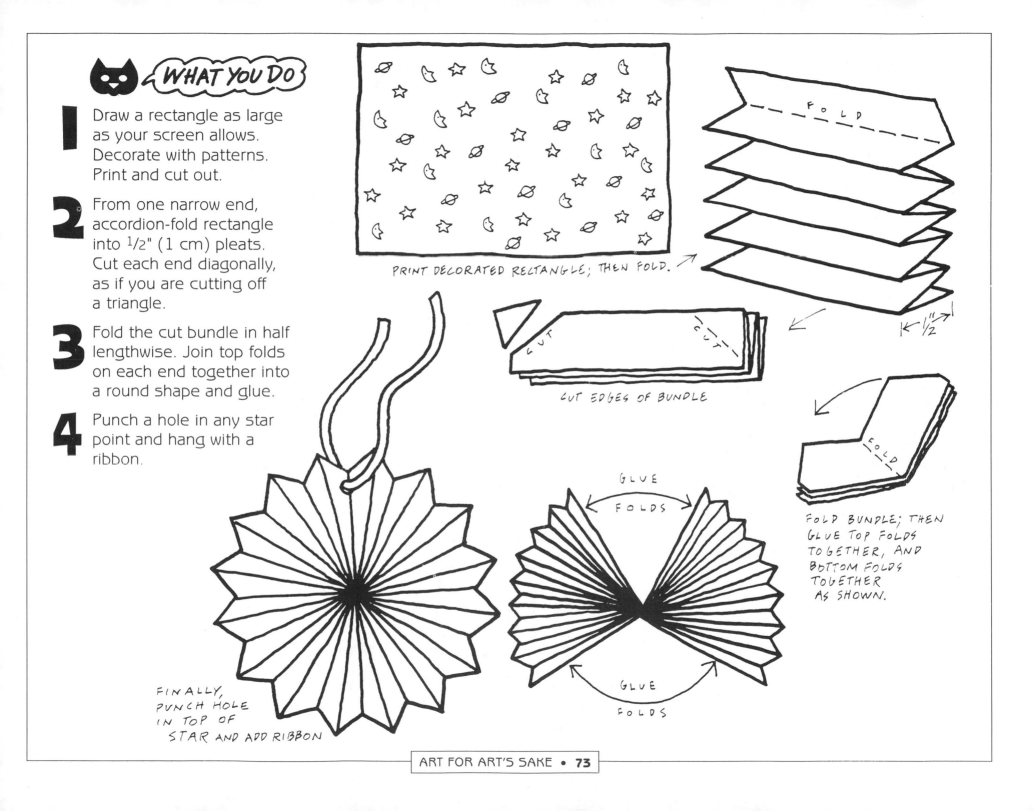

WHAT YOU DO

1 Draw a rectangle as large as your screen allows. Decorate with patterns. Print and cut out.

2 From one narrow end, accordion-fold rectangle into 1/2" (1 cm) pleats. Cut each end diagonally, as if you are cutting off a triangle.

3 Fold the cut bundle in half lengthwise. Join top folds on each end together into a round shape and glue.

4 Punch a hole in any star point and hang with a ribbon.

PRINT DECORATED RECTANGLE; THEN FOLD.

FOLD

1/2"

CUT EDGES OF BUNDLE

CUT

CUT

FOLD

FOLD BUNDLE; THEN GLUE TOP FOLDS TOGETHER, AND BOTTOM FOLDS TOGETHER AS SHOWN.

GLUE
FOLDS

GLUE
FOLDS

FINALLY, PUNCH HOLE IN TOP OF STAR AND ADD RIBBON

Fast, Faster, Fastest

The Cray supercomputer, the fastest computer built, is used for solving complex problems with very large numbers, such as astronomical studies and weather predictions. Incredibly, it can complete *billions* of calculations in seconds.

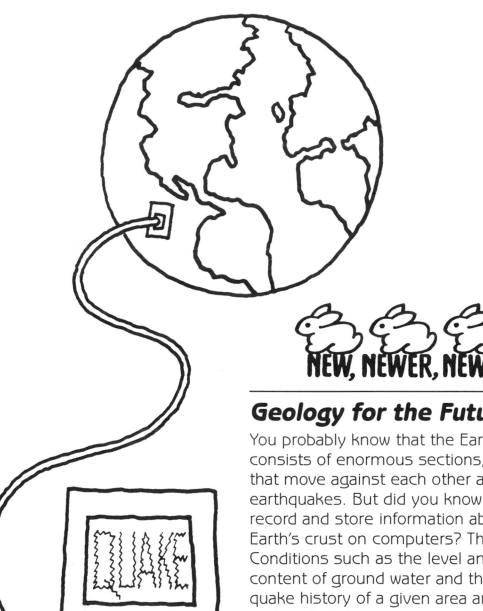

NEW, NEWER, NEWEST!

Geology for the Future

You probably know that the Earth's surface consists of enormous sections, or plates, that move against each other and create earthquakes. But did you know geologists record and store information about the Earth's crust on computers? That's right! Conditions such as the level and chemical content of ground water and the earthquake history of a given area are computer-analyzed, giving scientists valuable information for predicting future earthquakes.

The First "Real" Computer

Built in 1946 for the US military, ENIAC — a programmable calculator — is considered the first computer ever developed. Using thousands of vacuum tubes, it could add 5,000 numbers in one second. Today, computers can do millions of operations in seconds!

Can an IBM Read a Macintosh Disk?

Current computers and conversion software packages do allow users to read both Macintosh® and IBM compatible disks on their personal computers. But, you need to have the right computer or the proper software to do this. Look for increasing interchangability between Macintosh® — and DOS-based systems.

BIRD MOBILE

With this mobile, birds of a feather will surely flock together! Hang near a breezy spot and watch your birds move in the wind. Put folded wings at the rear of the bird for peacock or turkey tail feathers.

WHAT YOU NEED

Drinking straw

Ribbon

Scissors

Colored printer paper

Glue stick

WHAT YOU DO

1 To make wing, draw a 6" × 4" (15 × 10 cm) rectangle. Print 3 copies and cut out.

2 Draw the body outline about 6" × 3" (15 × 7.5 cm). Add an eye and a 1/2" (1 cm) line where the wing will join the body. Decorate body with designs and patterns. Print 3 copies and cut out. Cut slot on 1/2" (1 cm) line.

3 Fold wing pieces, starting from the narrow side, into 1/2" (1 cm) pleats, accordion-style. Fold each piece lengthwise, so when pinched at center, sides spring up.

DECORATE AND PRINT 3 COPIES OF BIRD

SLOT

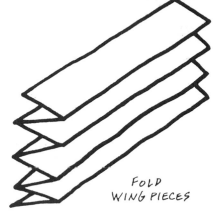

FOLD WING PIECES

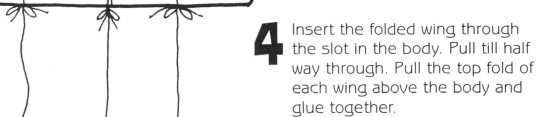

8"   12"   8"

ASSEMBLE MOBILE

PUT WING THROUGH SLOT

SLOT

4 Insert the folded wing through the slot in the body. Pull till half way through. Pull the top fold of each wing above the body and glue together.

5 Make a small hole at the top of wing assembly. Repeat for other two birds.

6 For mobile: Cut two 8" (20 cm) string pieces to be tied at each end of straw and one 12" (30 cm) piece to be tied in the middle. Tie other ends through the bird wing holes. Attach another length of string to the middle of the straw and hang.

SWAN LAKE SNOWFLAKE

Make your own snowstorm with a snowflake-filled window.
Create other designs to use as holiday ornaments.

WHAT YOU NEED

Scissors

Ribbon

Toothpick or hole punch

 **WHAT YOU DO**

1 Draw a large square and divide it into 4 equal squares.

2 Draw a diagonal line in the lower right section.

3 Draw the outline of a swan within the small left triangle that now exists, so parts of the picture touch the triangle's edges.

4 Print 1 copy and cut out the large square. Fold paper twice, leaving square with swan on top. Make one more fold along the diagonal line, leaving a triangle with the swan on top.

5 Carefully cut out the swan *from all the layers at once*. Leave the areas that touch the edge of the square and the diagonal line uncut. Push a toothpick through all layers to make an eye.

6 Unfold the layers to reveal a ring of swans. Hang with ribbon.

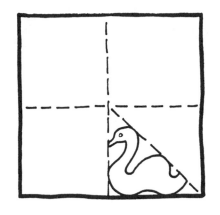

FOLD

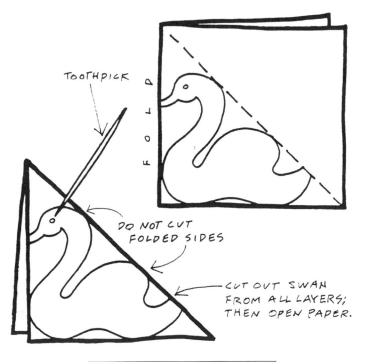

TOOTHPICK

FOLD

DO NOT CUT FOLDED SIDES

CUT OUT SWAN FROM ALL LAYERS; THEN OPEN PAPER.

 INSIDE THE COMPUTER

Sending Letters Without Stamps

Electronic mail, or e-mail, is one popular way people use the Internet. As with regular mail, you need the address of the person you are writing. If you want to send e-mail, you need to subscribe to an Internet server such as America OnLine®, Prodigy®, or Compuserve®. You also need a modem to attach your computer to a phone line. Sending e-mail is easy: Access your server's e-mail mode. Then type the address and your message in the area provided.

Sending a message: If you have the set-up for e-mail at home or at school, send me a message, if it is okay with a grown-up. I would love to hear from you! Here's my e-mail address:

Sabbeth@aol com

PATTERNED QUILT

Sewing a quilt has never been so easy! Make a watercolor pattern quilt, or try a theme quilt using African jungle animals!

WHAT YOU NEED

4 sheets white printer paper,
8 1/2" x 11" (21 cm x 27.5 cm)

Markers, several colors

Glue stick

Scissors

Construction paper, any color

Ribbon

WHAT YOU DO

1 Using markers (not crayons), color each sheet of white paper with a different repeating pattern — anything from flowers to stars to jungle animals.

2 Design a quilt pattern on the computer. Using a dashed line, draw a 4" (10 cm) square on the computer screen for each quilt square. Using a thicker line, draw two diagonal lines on the square, from corner to corner.

DECORATE SHEETS OF PAPER WITH REPEATING PATTERNS

DESIGN A QUILT PATTERN AND PRINT ON EACH PATTERN SHEET. CUT OUT TRIANGLES.

GLUE TRIANGLE ON CONSTRUCTION PAPER

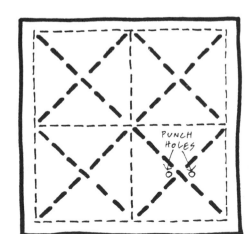 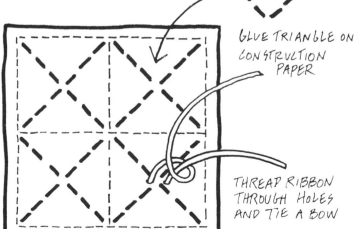

PUNCH HOLES

THREAD RIBBON THROUGH HOLES AND TIE A BOW

3 Now, put the patterned sheets (step #1) into your printer, making sure the quilt squares will print on the patterned side. Print 4 quilted squares, one on each patterned sheet.

4 Cut each patterned square along the outside, just outside the dashed line.

5 Now, cut each square into 4 triangles by cutting along the center of the thick diagonal lines.

6 Mix and match the patterned triangles back into squares. Arrange and glue onto a 9" (22.5 cm) square piece of construction paper, leaving a 1/2" (1 cm) border around the outside.

7 Punch 2 small holes in the center of the lower right square. Thread and tie a length of ribbon into a bow.

OCTOPUS'S GARDEN SPONGE ART

Make a set of pictures that tells an underwater story. After you draw and print the first scene, drag the sea creatures to different spots. Print each new scene as it tells a bit of the story. Then, add sponge art. Perhaps your octopus will end up kissing a fish — or eating it!

WHAT YOU NEED

Clean household sponge

Scissors

Tempera paint

Construction paper

Glue stick, markers

 **WHAT YOU DO**

1 Draw an underwater scene with an octopus, starfish, marine plants, and other ocean life. Print out and color.

2 On a sponge, draw a simple outline of a fish. Cut out.

3 Dip sponge into paint and make a fish print on your picture. When dry, add details such as eyes and gills. To frame, cut out and glue onto a larger piece of construction paper.

PRINT OUT UNDERWATER SCENE AND COLOR

DRAW OUTLINE OF FISH ON SPONGE

DIP FISH-SHAPED SPONGE IN PAINT AND PRESS ON UNDERWATER PRINT

How Long Do Floppies Last?

Floppy disks should last a very, very long time, if handled and stored properly. Remember to never handle your disks with sticky fingers. Always keep disks away from heat. Magnets will erase the data on a disk, so keep floppies away from magnets, as well as telephones or any electronic device.

Keeping floppies organized: A box of new disks comes with different colored labels. When you put a label on a floppy, place the color swatch so it appears at the top of the disk and wrap around the back side. Neatly print a description of what is on your disk with a felt-tip marker. Then, organize your disks by color, such as red labels for homework, blue for artwork, and store your disks with the color side up. You'll find each subject in a snap!

Check It Out!

Does your grocery store use computers at the checkout counter? Before computers, clerks had to punch prices on the cash register's keys.

Today, clerks pass items over scanners. The code printed on the package indicates the name, size, and price of the product which prints out on the receipt. Some registers even call out the price aloud! The computer also keeps track of what is sold, helping the store manager decide when to re-order.

CREATIVE PLAY

You don't need a hammer or nails or any other fancy stuff to make great toys! With just a little imagination, a few pieces of paper, and your computer, you can create a whole box of homemade treasures.

SOAPY SAILBOAT

Make two of these soap boats and invite a friend to a race across the bathtub. Just use paper plates to create wind. Ahoy!

WHAT YOU DO

1 Draw a 4" (10 cm) square on your screen for a sail. Decorate it as you wish.

2 Draw a 3" (7.5 cm) figure for the boat's captain. Print and cut out the sail and your figure.

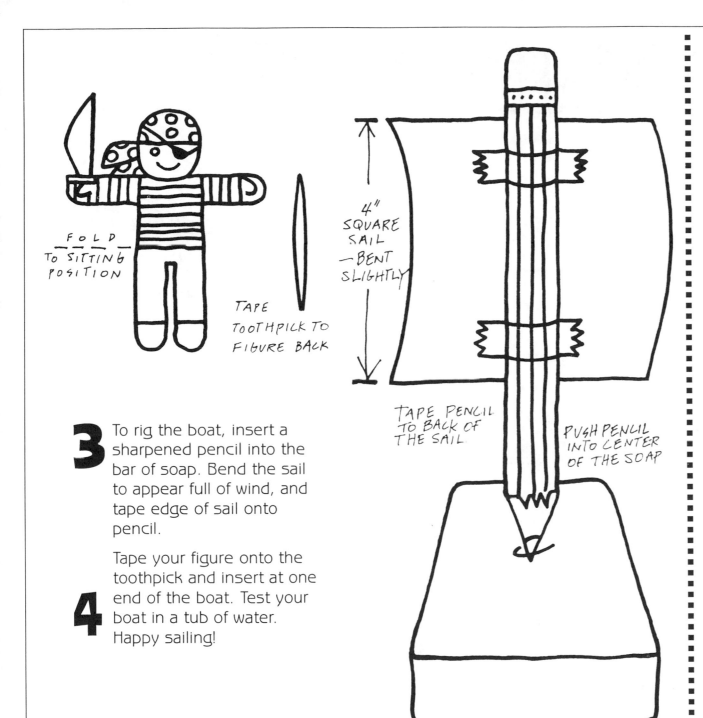

FOLD TO SITTING POSITION

TAPE TOOTHPICK TO FIGURE BACK

4" SQUARE SAIL —BENT SLIGHTLY

TAPE PENCIL TO BACK OF THE SAIL

PUSH PENCIL INTO CENTER OF THE SOAP

3 To rig the boat, insert a sharpened pencil into the bar of soap. Bend the sail to appear full of wind, and tape edge of sail onto pencil.

4 Tape your figure onto the toothpick and insert at one end of the boat. Test your boat in a tub of water. Happy sailing!

Will "Rebooting" Hurt My Computer?

Spend a little time at a computer and you'll discover how a screen can sometimes just freeze up. Tapping the right keys or clicking the pointer doesn't help. When this happens, turning the computer completely off and on (called rebooting) may be tempting, but this could really harm your computer. Instead, do a *warm boot*. On Macintosh®, hold down the Control and Command keys while pressing the start-up button on the top of the keyboard. On DOS computers, press the reset button. If still no luck, ask a grown-up for help.

CLOTHESPIN PEOPLE

Make a cast of clothespin characters from your favorite story. Use them as puppets and put on a show for your family or friends.

WHAT YOU NEED

Wooden clothespins

Popsicle sticks

Markers, several colors

Scissors

Glue

 **WHAT YOU DO**

1 To make person: Cut a Popsicle stick into thirds. Use the rounded edge pieces for arms. Glue arms, rounded side down, at each side of clothespin.

2 Draw faces and hair for each person.

3 Design clothes and costumes. You'll need a front and a back for each piece. Draw a dress front, then copy it and paste a duplicate. Decorate the duplicate as the dress back. Create shirts, overalls, and trousers, too. For a ballerina, draw toe shoes.

4 Print, color, and cut out. Glue clothing to each clothespin person.

CUT POPSICLE STICK INTO 1/3 PIECES

ARM | ARM

GLUE ARM TO BODY

DRAW FACE AND HAIR

A Prehistoric Computer

Thousands of years ago, people were creating tools for calculating all sorts of things. For instance, it was important to know when the planting season started. In Salisbury, England there's a circle of huge stones over 4,000 years old, called Stonehenge, which some experts think is a kind of prehistoric computer. Ancient peoples may have placed the stones so that the sun cast a shadow in a way that revealed which season it was.

JACK-IN-A BOX

This age-old toy is sure to deliver a surprise to anyone who opens it! For a different pop-out treat, type a special message such as "Happy Birthday, David" and then give as a gift. Hide a few treats inside for a surprise!

WHAT YOU NEED

Tape

Scissors

Markers, several colors

 **WHAT YOU DO**

1 Jack's box: Draw six 1½"
(3.5 cm) squares as shown.
Add tabs.

2 Decorate your squares with
patterns and small drawings.
Print and cut out.

3 To draw Jack, draw a
rectangle, about ½" x 5"
(1 cm x 12.5 cm). Draw
a face and hat at the top.
Print and cut out.

4 To assemble, fold box along
each edge of square and tabs.
Tape bottom and side tabs on
inside of box, but not the top.

5 To make Jack spring from
his box, accordion-fold the
rectangle below the face. Tape
the bottom of accordion to
inside bottom of the box.

6 Push the folded figure into
the box and shut lid.

Tricks of the trade: Here's
a quick way to draw Jack's
box. On Macintosh, select the
rectangle tool; then hold your
Shift key down and draw a
square about 1½" (3.5 cm)
wide. Holding the Shift key
while using the rectangle tool
will create a perfect square!
Copy this square, and then
paste it 5 times into the
correct positions. Add the
tabs and decorations. For
Windows®, hold down either
the Shift or Control key
(which key to hold depends
on the program) while drawing
a square.

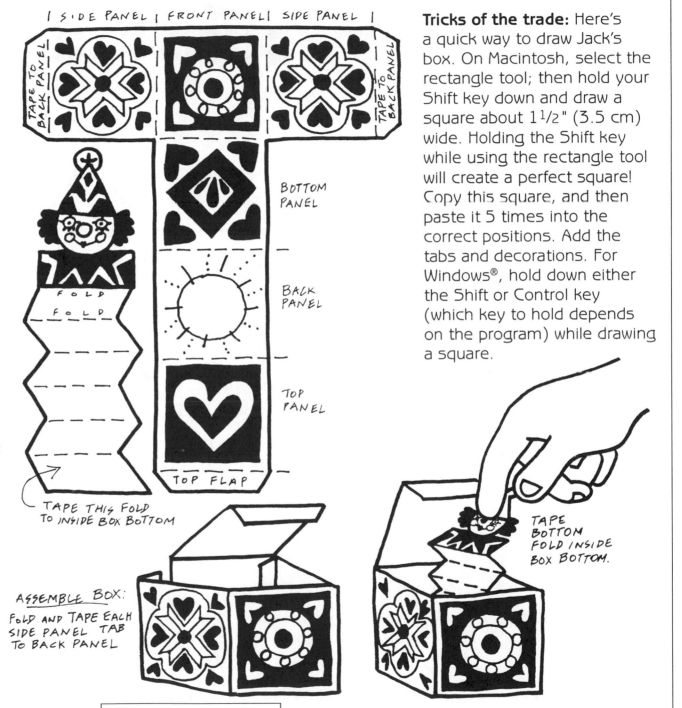

STOP MOUSING AROUND

Your mouse is a big help most of the time, but did you know your computer is also full of great keyboard shortcuts? Try these and see!

For Macintosh® Users:

Copy: Hold down the Command key, which has an apple on it, while pressing "C."

Paste: Hold down the Command key while pressing "V."

Cut: Hold down the Command key and press "X."

Cancel: Hold down the Command key and press "Z" to cancel or "undo" your previous action.

For Windows® Users:

Copy: Hold down the Control key while pressing the C key.

Paste: Hold down the Control key while pressing the V key.

Cut: Hold down the Control key while pressing the X key.

Undo: Hold down the Control key while pressing the Z key.

"Click" Art

Not everyone can draw a scene that looks exactly like the real thing. Yet, sometimes people need this type of artwork to illustrate a story or advertisement. For this reason, artists decided to make books of drawings to sell to people. When a piece of art was needed, it was "clipped" out of a book and used. Today, *clip art* or *"click" art* (cut out with the click of a mouse) is available on disk. With click art, artists can start with a simple click art drawing and add their own touches for a personalized piece.

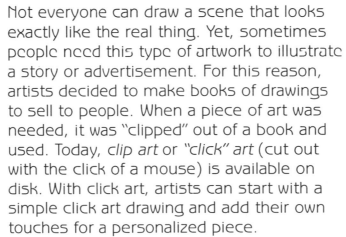

Explore your clip art cabinet: Some computers come loaded with clip art. For Macintosh®, it's found in the scrapbook. Some people buy additional software with plenty of clip art on it. Find out about your computer's click art capabilities!

MAGIC TRICK

Calling all magicians! Here's a great trick that's sure to confuse your friends. Look in a magic trick book for ideas for a whole magic show. Think of a stage name, such as The Great Mysto, and make flyers and tickets for your show!

 **WHAT YOU DO**

1 Draw a rectangle, 5" x 2" (12.5 cm x 5 cm). Decorate with magical pictures and mysterious sayings.

2 Print and cut out. Color with markers.

3 Accordion-fold the rectangle into thirds. Attach a paper clip near a fold so it grips the loose end to the fold. Put the other clip at the other end so it, too, grips a fold to a loose end.

4 Grip the loose ends and pull away from each other.

5 Presto! The clips are linked together. (If the clips are attached near the ends but over the folds, they'll simply fly off the paper when the ends are pulled apart.)

2"

1 ⁵⁄₈"

5"

ACCORDION-FOLD RECTANGLE INTO THIRDS

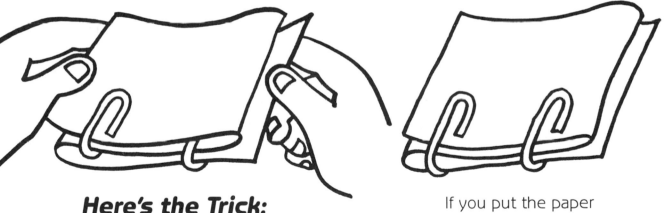

Here's the Trick:

Put the paper clips on this way and they will link when you pull the ends apart!

If you put the paper clips on this way, they will slide off unlinked when you pull on the ends.

WEATHER VANE

Start your own weather station with a homemade weather vane!
Add a rain gauge by making inch marks on a tall glass. Then add
an outdoor thermometer and give daily weather reports.

 **WHAT YOU NEED**

Colored printer paper
Pencil, glue stick
Scissors
Styrofoam block, 1" (2.5 cm) cube (reuse from computer packing box)
Empty thread spool
Masking tape
Poster board

Every little breeze points me with ease

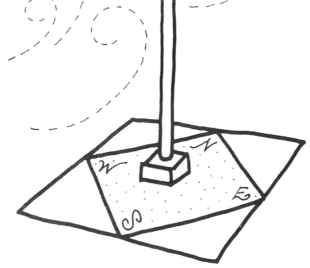

 **WHAT YOU DO**

1 For the base, draw a 4¹⁄₂" (11 cm) square. Using your line tool, draw a diamond inside the first square. Type the letters N, E, S, and W at each diamond point. Print 1 copy and cut out along outer square.

2 Draw a directional arrow, about 7" (17.5 cm) long and 2" (5 cm) tall. Decorate with pictures or a short message. Print 1 copy and cut out.

3 From poster board, cut out a same-sized square (step #1) and a same-sized arrow (step #2). Glue poster-board backing to base.

4 Glue square to the styrofoam in the center of the base. Gently push the pencil into the styrofoam so it fits snugly and stands up.

Hint: Make the hole with a sharpened pencil point, then push into place, eraser side down.

5 Sandwich spool between both arrows with tape. Tape top of spool. Place spool hole over the pencil tip so arrow moves freely.

6 Position the base of the weather vane so each letter faces the correct direction. The arrow will point in the direction from which the wind blows.

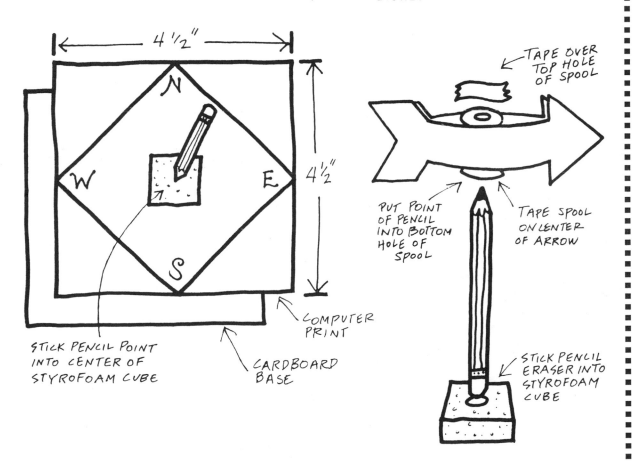

4 1/2"

4 1/2"

N

W

E

S

COMPUTER PRINT

STICK PENCIL POINT INTO CENTER OF STYROFOAM CUBE

CARDBOARD BASE

TAPE OVER TOP HOLE OF SPOOL

PUT POINT OF PENCIL INTO BOTTOM HOLE OF SPOOL

TAPE SPOOL ON CENTER OF ARROW

STICK PENCIL ERASER INTO STYROFOAM CUBE

Weather Watch

For over 200 years, farmers used weather vanes to determine wind direction. Today, computers help meteorologists (people who study weather patterns and predict weather) determine what weather to expect. In fact, modern weather-forecasting would be impossible without computers, because weather forecasters handle huge amounts of data received from ground stations, satellites, weather balloons, and more. And to be accurate, the data must be processed very quickly — something computers do best!

SOLAR SYSTEM MOBILE

Create the night sky right in your own bedroom! Hang this solar system mobile from the ceiling and place sticker stars on the walls for a bedroom planetarium!

WHAT YOU DO

1 Draw a large circle in the center of your screen. Add sunglasses and sunshine rays, then print 2 copies. Cut out.

2 Draw a circle for each of the 9 planets. Decorate each and type in each planet's name. Draw each planet's size in proportion to the others as follows: Jupiter the largest, then Saturn, Uranus, Neptune, Earth, Venus, Mars, Mercury, and Pluto.

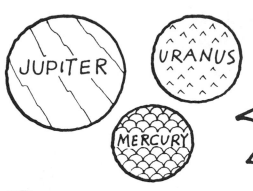

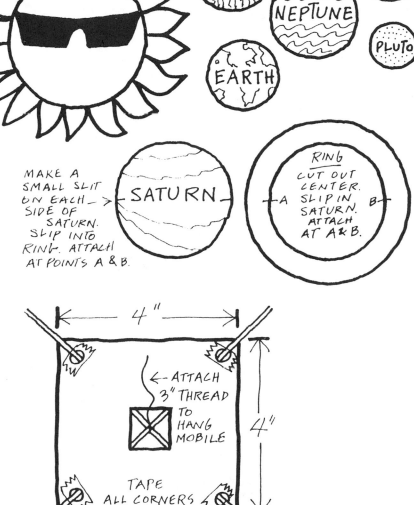

JUPITER

URANUS

MERCURY

MARS

NEPTUNE

VENUS

PLUTO

EARTH

3 To make Saturn's ring, copy and paste Saturn's circle. Place the new circle aside and draw a larger circle around it. Print 1 copy of the ring; 2 copies of each planet. Cut out.

4 Cut ten 10" (25 cm) lengths of thread and sandwich between each planet's double circle (front and back) with glue. Repeat for the sun. Slide Saturn's ring around its shape.

5 To make the support, cut the cardboard into a 4" (10 cm) square. Poke a hole in each corner and in the center. Slide wire pieces diagonally through holes and tape. Hang a 3' (90 cm) length of thread from the center of the support to hang from ceiling.

6 Suspend sun and planets from the 2 wire pieces.

MAKE A SMALL SLIT ON EACH SIDE OF SATURN. SLIP INTO RING. ATTACH AT POINTS A & B.

SATURN

RING
CUT OUT CENTER. SLIP IN SATURN. ATTACH AT A & B.
A — B

4"

4"

← ATTACH 3" THREAD TO HANG MOBILE

TAPE ALL CORNERS

TOP VIEW SUPPORT

Computerized Filing Cabinet

The *hard disk*, or *hard drive*, of your computer is like a big filing cabinet where all your software programs are stored. As you save new documents, they are stored in this "cabinet," until you call them up again. The nice thing is that things are always where you left them!

MEDIEVAL CASTLE

Create an entire kingdom right on your computer! Paint a moat on poster board and add a drawbridge. Then, draw a dragon and knights, cut out, and place outside your castle.

WHAT YOU DO

1 To make castle pattern, draw a rectangle about 2½" x 6" (6 cm x 15 cm). Add ½" (1 cm) boxes along the top of it. Print 5 copies.

2 Using the castle pattern as a base, make several turrets. Decorate with windows, window boxes, a large front entry door, and knights in armor, a prince and princess. Print at least 5 decorations.

3 Cut out the turret pieces. To make outer wall, glue 4 pieces end to end, making a very large ring. For a tower, stack 3 pieces on top of each other and glue. Glue other pieces into small, individual rings.

4 To assemble castle: Stand tower inside your outer wall. Cut two 1" (2.5 cm) slots in each turret bottom, then slide slots over top of outer wall or tower.

How RAM Works

RAM, or *random access memory*, is the active part of a computer's memory. When a software program is used, it has to be loaded into this memory system for the computer to use it.

RAM is a lot like the top of your desk. As you open files, your desk starts to fill up. Eventually, your desk gets too full for more files, so you have to put some work away to make room. This is how your RAM works, too. If you have a small amount of RAM, you have a small desk. If you try to open several files at the same time, your computer will tell you eventually that there is no more memory. Closing files and "quitting" software programs that you are no longer using will leave plenty of RAM available.

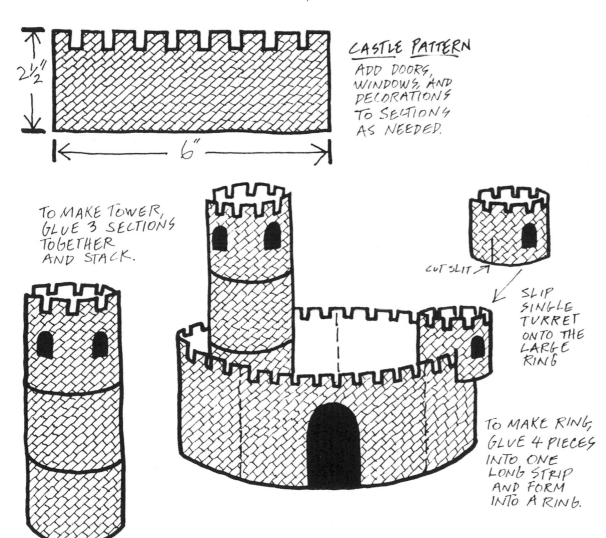

CASTLE PATTERN
ADD DOORS, WINDOWS, AND DECORATIONS TO SECTIONS AS NEEDED.

2½"

6"

TO MAKE TOWER, GLUE 3 SECTIONS TOGETHER AND STACK.

CUT SLIT

SLIP SINGLE TURRET ONTO THE LARGE RING

TO MAKE RING, GLUE 4 PIECES INTO ONE LONG STRIP AND FORM INTO A RING.

 # MEDIEVAL DRAGON

Create a fearsome dragon to scare castle dwellers. Or, make unicorns, giant horses, and other animal shapes for a rowdy medieval zoo!

WHAT YOU NEED

Scissors
Colored printer paper
Markers
Glue stick

 ## WHAT YOU DO

1 Draw a horizontal line across the middle of your drawing area to divide the dragon in two. Draw a long oval about 1/2" (1 cm) below the line for the dragon's body.

2 Add a tail to one side of the body. To make its spikes, draw triangles along the dragon's back and tail so some spikes touch the horizontal line. Add the head, as shown.

3 Draw two feet as separate pieces. Make a long flame for a fire-breathing dragon, and add scales or patterns to its body, if you wish.

4 Print 1 copy of all the pieces.

5 Before cutting, fold the dragon body along the horizontal line. Cut out the body, but leave the triangles on the fold attached. Cut the head from the bottom so the neck stays attached to the closest triangle. If you make a mistake, just print another copy and try again!

6 Cut out the feet, snipping slots. Slide each body side into one of the slots, positioning the feet so the dragon can stand. Bend its head down or to one side.

7 Cut out flame, color it red, and glue to the dragon's snout.

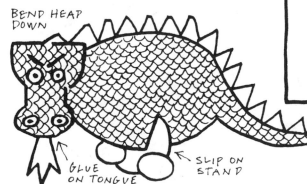

BEND HEAP DOWN

GLUE ON TONGUE

SLIP ON STAND

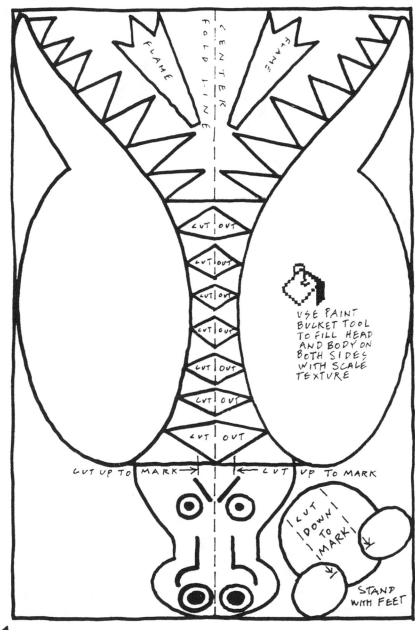

FLAME

CENTER FOLD LINE

FLAME

CUT OUT

CUT OUT

CUT OUT

CUT OUT

CUT OUT

CUT OUT

CUT OUT

USE PAINT BULKET TOOL TO FILL HEAD AND BODY ON BOTH SIDES WITH SCALE TEXTURE

CUT UP TO MARK → ← CUT UP TO MARK

CUT DOWN TO MARK

STAND WITH FEET

COMPUTER Q&A

What Is GUI?

If you own a Macintosh®, you know how incredibly "user-friendly" these machines are. That's because the creators of Macintosh® thought it very important to make a computer that was easy to use — for everyone! They were the first to use pull-down menus and icons, instead of cumbersome keyboard codes. This technology, called *GUI* for *G*raphic *U*ser *I*nterface, is pronounced just like the word for a sticky mess — gooey!

A few years ago, DOS computers added user-friendly software, too, called Windows®. It uses GUI technology and allows users to access icons and menus in ways much like a Macintosh®.

Then & Now

Strike Up the Band!

Imagine writing 1,000 musical compositions for entire orchestras and other musicians by hand. Incredibly, that's exactly what Wolfgang Amadeus Mozart did during the course of his short life! He carefully wrote down music for all the performers of a piece, including singers, conductor, and instrumentalists. Often composers gave their hand-written music to the orchestra just in time for a concert. In dim candlelight, the players had a tough job reading the hastily scrawled markings!

Today, composers can link an electronic keyboard to a computer and play music while the computer "writes" it down! Special software even allows the computer to write the correct pitches and rhythms. Imagine how helpful this would have been to Mozart!

GOOD TIME CELEBRATIONS

No matter what you are celebrating — a birthday, the first day of summer, having your soccer team over for a barbecue — half the fun of gathering friends and family together is getting ready for their arrival! Here are plenty of ideas to liven up the festivities using computer creations! There's a whole afternoon's worth of ideas to help you have fun!

LADYBUG NAPKIN RINGS

★★★

Legend has it that ladybugs bring good luck to those they land on.
Celebrate a year of good fortune using these ladybug napkin rings
when setting the table for dinner — or at a picnic with your friends.

WHAT YOU NEED

Glue stick

Scissors

Paper clips

Markers, black and red

Garbage bag twist ties

WHAT YOU DO

Draw a rectangular strip, about 1" x 6" (2.5 cm x 15 cm). Draw a ladybug in the center of the strip with its body extending out above and below the rectangle. Fill in solid black for the ladybug's head, shell dots, and wing divider. Using white paper, print one copy for each guest.

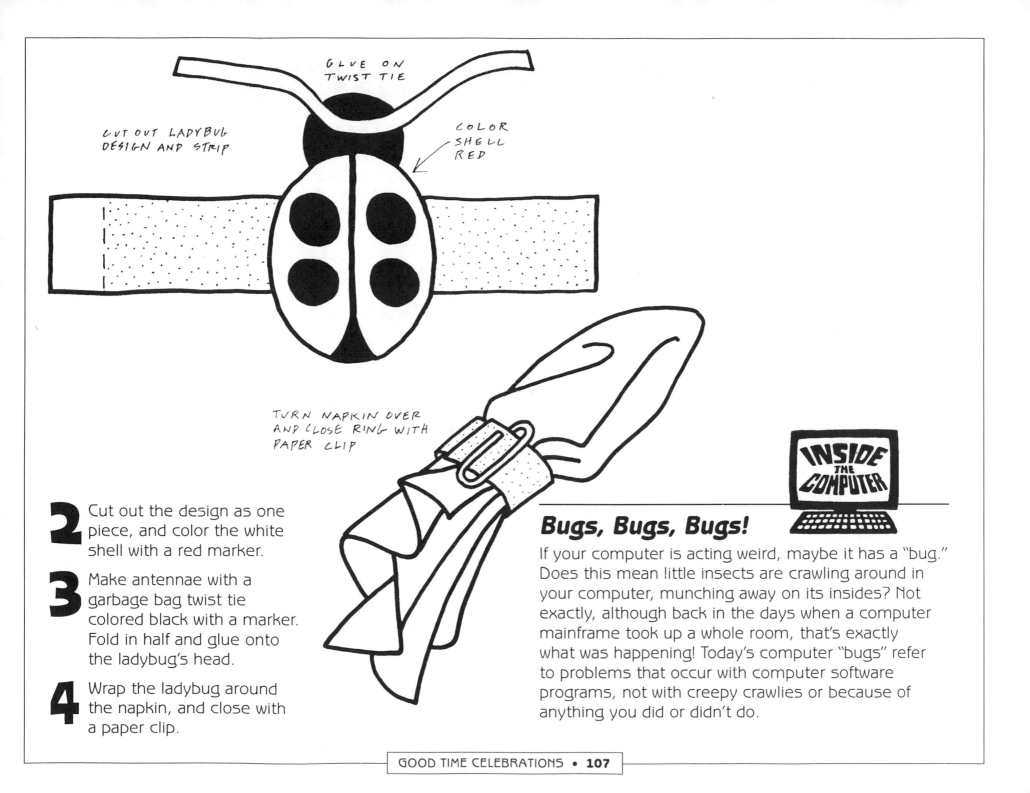

GLUE ON
TWIST TIE

CUT OUT LADYBUG
DESIGN AND STRIP

COLOR
SHELL
RED

TURN NAPKIN OVER
AND CLOSE RING WITH
PAPER CLIP

2 Cut out the design as one piece, and color the white shell with a red marker.

3 Make antennae with a garbage bag twist tie colored black with a marker. Fold in half and glue onto the ladybug's head.

4 Wrap the ladybug around the napkin, and close with a paper clip.

INSIDE THE COMPUTER

Bugs, Bugs, Bugs!

If your computer is acting weird, maybe it has a "bug." Does this mean little insects are crawling around in your computer, munching away on its insides? Not exactly, although back in the days when a computer mainframe took up a whole room, that's exactly what was happening! Today's computer "bugs" refer to problems that occur with computer software programs, not with creepy crawlies or because of anything you did or didn't do.

FLOWERPOT SURPRISE

****

You don't need a special occasion to enjoy these flowerpots — any old day will do! Make several flowers of different colors and shapes for people in your family, for party favors — or to give to a neighbor who needs cheering up.

WHAT YOU NEED

- Green pipe cleaners
- Small flowerpots
- Jelly beans or unshelled peanuts
- Scissors
- Colored printer paper
- Glue stick

Mom   Mom   Dad   Dad

1 Draw a medium-sized circle in the center of your screen.

Hint: Hold down the Shift or Control key while drawing to make a circle.

2 Draw petals around the circle, and add a face to the inside. Print 2 different-colored copies of the flower for each place holder.

3 Draw 2 leaves and type a name in each leaf. Repeat for each name. Print on green paper.

4 Divide printed flowers into 2 equal sets. Cut out the circles of one set and glue them onto the center of a second set, covering their circles. For instance, a purple flower may have a pink center. Discard the remaining outer pieces of flowers.

5 Place each glued flower on top of a blank sheet, the same color as the flower front.

6 Cut out the flower shape from the sheet.

7 Glue flower front and back together with a pipe cleaner sandwiched for a stem.

8 Make two branches by twisting a shorter pipe cleaner around the stem. Glue 1 leaf on each branch.

9 Twist the "stem" into a ring and set into a flowerpot. Fill pot with jelly beans or unshelled peanuts.

PLACE FLOWER ON BLANK SHEET AND CUT OUT

GLUE DIFFERENT COLOR FACE ON FLOWER

PRINT LEAVES WITH NAMES ON GREEN PAPER

Mom Mom

GLUE FLOWER BACK TO FLOWER FRONT WITH PIPE CLEANER INBETWEEN

FLOWER BACK

FLOWER FRONT

TWIST SHORT PIPE CLEANER AROUND STEM AND GLUE ON LEAVES

Mom Mom

TWIST STEM INTO RING AND PUT INTO A FLOWERPOT

BUZZING BEE

★★

Invite these musical bees to your next picnic, or tape one onto a surprise birthday gift for a friend!

WHAT YOU NEED

Glue stick

Scissors

Yellow printer paper

Drinking straw

WHAT YOU DO

1 Draw a bee about the size of your thumb, and then add wings. Print 2 copies on yellow paper and cut out.

2 Place the pieces back to back, with design facing out. Sandwich one end of a drinking straw between the pieces and glue, leaving the mouth end and wings unglued. Fold the wings up so they look like they're fluttering.

3 Make your bee buzz by humming into the open end of the straw. Tap your finger over the bee's mouth for different sounds.

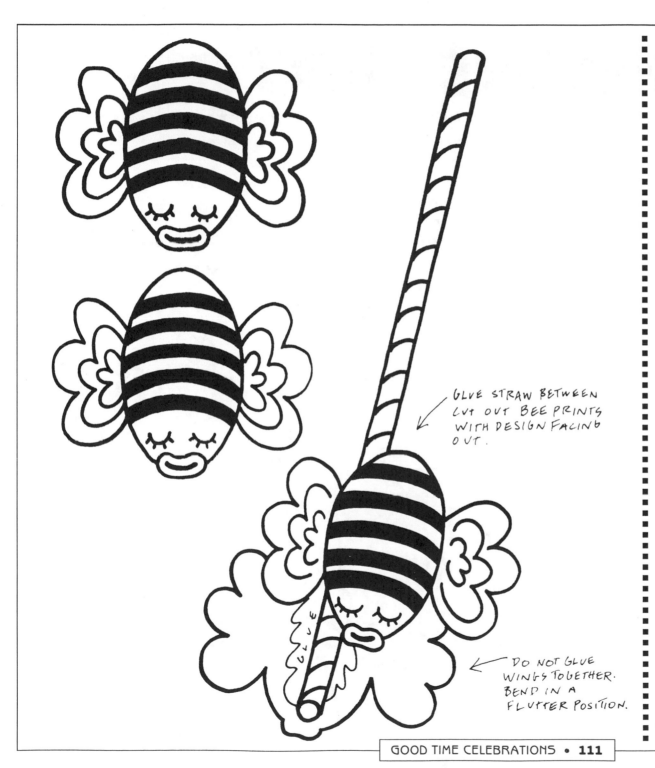

GLUE STRAW BETWEEN CUT OUT BEE PRINTS WITH DESIGN FACING OUT.

DO NOT GLUE WINGS TOGETHER. BEND IN A FLUTTER POSITION.

NEW, NEWER, NEWEST!

Keeping Our Roads Safe

Next time you're in a car, notice how long you and other cars stop at traffic lights — there's almost a rhythm to the way everyone moves about, isn't there? That's because traffic engineers use computers to keep traffic moving smoothly and safely. By counting the number of cars and trucks with electronic sensors, engineers can decide how to time traffic lights along a busy street.

TREASURE HUNT

★★

Half the fun of treasure hunts is in making them up, and with your computer, you can create all kinds of hunts. Try a themed hunt or an alphabet hunt where you are in search of items starting with the last seven letters of the alphabet. A number hunt might involve adding, subtracting, and multiplying! For extra fun, make a picture hunt for preschoolers who can't yet read, drawing the picture of what they are to find.

WHAT YOU NEED

Colored printer paper

Pencils

 **WHAT YOU DO**

1. Make a list of 10 – 15 items to search for as treasures. For an Indoor Treasure Hunt, you might include items such as a red shoe, a pink comb, or a wooden spoon. Next to the name of each treasure, draw a long line where you will record where you spotted the treasure. (Please leave the treasure where you see it.) Print out one list for each player.

2. You can have a treasure hunt where you search for "hidden" treasures placed by a grown-up, or you can search for items usually found in and around a house, such as a dirty red sock or a pink bar of soap.

3. You can also hunt as individual players, form two teams, or hunt with a partner.

4. Set some rules such as how far you can roam — in three rooms, around the yard, in the park, or wherever. Also set a time limit. First player or team to locate all the items wins!

Treasure Hunt

1. Spoon _____
2. Paper Clip _____
3. Shoe _____
4. Clothespin _____
5. Carrot _____
6. Sock _____
7. Toothbrush _____
8. Newspaper _____
9. Earring _____
10. Paintbrush _____
11. Birthday Candle _____
12. Toothpick _____
13. Comb _____
14. Balloon _____

 **COMPUTER Q&A**

Will Audio CDs Work On Computer?

Thanks to some terrific technology, it's possible to play your favorite audio CDs on your CD-equipped computer. You can even purchase some very good speakers to plug into your computer. Write a letter to your best friend while listening to your favorite musical group, or do homework on the computer while enjoying Vivaldi's *Four Seasons*. If your computer has a CD-ROM drive, the world of music is at your finger-tips!

Multimedia Mania

Multimedia PCs do amazing things! They expand the capability of computers with CD-ROM drives, fax/modems, speakers, and sound capability. They may be able to connect video camcorders to the computer, so that video can be recorded on the hard drive. Just think, you could watch your video-taped birthday party on the computer!

What Is CD-ROM?

Would you believe that an entire encyclopedia can be stored on a single CD-ROM (Compact Disc — Read-Only Memory) disc? It's true! To use a CD-ROM disc, you need a CD-ROM disc drive. Some computers come with this drive built inside. A CD-ROM disc is different from a floppy disk in that you can only get information *from* a CD-ROM, you can't put new information *onto* it. And, a CD-ROM has much more memory than a floppy disk. You would need 450 floppy disks to hold as much information as 1 CD-ROM!

Good clean fun: Have you ever put a CD-ROM disc in your CD-ROM drive only to find that your computer couldn't read it? If so, check your CD for dirt. Just hold the disc by its edges and turn it over. Are there finger-prints, dust particles, or smudges on the shiny silver surface? Ask a grown-up if you can wipe away the grime from the center outward with a very soft cloth. Keeping your CDs stored in their cases will help you avoid smudges and accidental scratches, too.

Life Before PC

Before personal computers were available, typing anything from a letter to a book was a real chore. Errors were corrected with a pencil eraser (which sometimes tore the paper), or covered up with a white fluid. It was no small feat to type a letter without mistakes!

As you know, typing on a computer is very easy. Errors are corrected by pressing a delete or backspace key. Whole paragraphs can be moved around the page and you can add a new idea at any time. Spelling and even grammar can be checked with the push of a button.

Exploring Your Options

Computers have an additional advantage. When you look at your keyboard, you see many letters, numbers, and symbols. But can you think of any symbols that don't appear on the keyboard? What if you need to type a cent (¢) sign? These additional symbols may be available if you know where to look for them. On a Macintosh®, these extra keys are called "keycaps" and they're found in the Desk Accessories. In Windows®, look for Character Map in the Accessories.

SiLLY WORD GAME

★★

This game is fun anytime. Put together a whole book of word games by writing several funny stories. Then give your book a title and design a cover for it.

WHAT YOU NEED

Colored printer paper

WHAT YOU DO

1 Think up a short, silly story. Choose a few important words in the story, then erase them, leaving a blank where the word should go. Decide whether the missing word is a noun, verb, adjective, or adverb (see page 118).

2 Type the story, including its blank lines, on the computer. Double space. Below each blank line, type what part of speech the missing word is.

3 Make a story about each of your friends. Add designs along the borders to illustrate your stories. Print one copy of each story.

4 Give your friends a story and a pencil. Be sure not to give them a story about themselves. Let each person fill in the story's blanks by calling out what type of word is needed (noun, verb, adjective, adverb). When completed, read each story aloud.

Athena was walking to the store one day to buy some _____ noun s when she ran into a purple _____ noun which resembled her best friend's _____ noun . Shocked, she _____ adverb ly whispered, "My, what a big _____ noun you have". To which it _____ verb ed and walked away.

PARTS OF SPEECH

Words go together to help you express ideas and feelings in a serious way or in a silly way. Try a game with a friend where you say a word like "three," and they say "adjective" and then use it in a sentence. "Would you believe that I saw three bears today?"

Nouns: A noun is a person, place, or thing. Words such as hippopotamus, barn, tree, and stream are all nouns.

Verbs: Verbs are action words; they tell what a noun does or what happens to it. Words such as tumble, gallop, gulp, and dance are all verbs.

Adverbs: Adverbs describe how, when, or where something occurs. Words such as quickly, secretly, soon, and ferociously are adverbs. (Notice that a lot of -ly words are adverbs.)

Adjectives: Adjectives describe nouns. Adjectives include words such as goofy, happy, round, and purple.

Built for Speed

Modern computers differ from earlier models in many important ways. Believe it or not, some early personal computers could only store about 340 typed pages of information. Today's models have storage capacity about 1000 times larger! The earliest systems could perform only 50 operations each second, but today's machines can do millions of operations per second.

Other marvelous modern features include the addition of sound to the personal computer, CD-ROM, and color monitors that can produce the same effect as color TV. And right now, Internet users can do library research and go shopping on-line. So what's ahead in computer technology? Many experts believe it won't be long before people use their computers to vote, file tax returns, and do banking right from their homes!

What's "Virtual Reality"?

Imagine being surrounded by your monitor's screen. Wherever you look, your computer projects an image on its screen of what you should see. Sound too real to be true? Well, that's exactly what virtual reality (VR) programs are like! With virtual reality you not only see but you also experience your environment. You could visit a museum of natural history via a VR-programmed computer. As you "enter" the museum on screen, you might look to the left and see a dinosaur skeleton. Straight ahead you might see a door that you could push open to enter the next room. VR users wear goggles and a glove so the computer "senses" which way a person is looking and reaching.

On exhibit: Your local science museum or computer store may have a virtual reality exhibit you could try out.

RIDDLE FORTUNE COOKIES

★★★

WHAT YOU NEED

Scissors

Fortune cookies
(see recipe, page 121)

*Stump your friends with tricky riddles!
Or, instead of typing words, use pictures
to send a fortune cookie message.*

WHAT YOU DO

1 Think of 8 riddles. Here are a few ideas to get you started:

Why was 6 afraid of 7?

Answer: Because 7, 8, 9!

What do you call the fear of tight chimneys?

Answer: Santa Claustrophobia!

What is a snake's favorite subject in school?

Answer: Hissssstory!

2 Type the riddles, one to a line, by clicking on the text tool in a painting program (it usually looks like a big A). Or, use a word processing program, such as MS Word® or Word-Perfect®. Type the question on one line, then add a design. Don't type the answers — only you will hold the key!

3 Print the questions, then cut into strips. Set aside to add to the cookies.

U ☆-st A GR8 ♡-H+ist

What is a snake's favorite subject in school?

Why was 6 afraid of 7??

FORTUNE COOKIE RECIPE

★★★

WHAT YOU NEED

¼ cup (50 ml) all-purpose flour
2 tablespoons (25 ml) sugar
1 tablespoon (15 ml) cornstarch
Dash of salt
2 tablespoons (25 ml) cooking oil
1 egg white
1 tablespoon (15 ml) water

WHAT YOU DO

1 In a small mixing bowl, stir together flour, sugar, cornstarch, and salt. Add oil and egg white; stir until smooth. Add water and mix well.

2 Ask a grown-up to help you pour about a tablespoon of batter onto a lightly greased skillet. Spread batter into about a 3½" (8.5 cm) circle. Cook over low heat about 4 minutes or until lightly browned. Flip cookie with wide spatula and cook for 1 minute more.

3 Working quickly, place cookie on a pot holder or paper towel. Put a riddle strip in the center (fold paper, if necessary). Fold cookie in half, then fold again over edge of a glass. Let cool. Repeat with remaining batter. Makes 8 cookies.

 # PIN-THE-NOSE ON THE CLOWN

★★★

*Send in the clowns! Then play this classic pin-the-nose game circus-style.
Don't wait for a birthday party! Play it any day you feel like celebrating!*

 ## WHAT YOU NEED

Poster board

Colored printer paper

Glue stick

Waxed paper

Scissors, tape

 ## WHAT YOU DO

■ Draw a clown face as large as possible on your computer. Put a circle where the nose should go. Print 3 copies on white paper. Then make various hats and wigs to dress the clowns. Print out on different colors of paper, and cut out.

GLUE CLOWN FACES
TO POSTER BOARD

MAKE HATS
AND WIGS.
CUT OUT
AND
GLUE ON
FACES.

CUT OUT CIRCLES
FOR PLAYER NOSE PIECES

Name

PRINT NAME
ON FRONT

PUT TAPE
ON BACK

2 Make a circle the size of the clown's nose. Copy and paste duplicates for all the players. Type each player's name on a nose. Print on bright pink or red paper, then cut out.

3 Put a piece of rolled tape on the back of each nose. Stick to a piece of waxed paper, until it is the player's turn.

PUT
NOSE
PIECES
ON
WAXED
PAPER

Pam   Greg

Patty   Steve

4 Glue the clown pieces to a piece of brightly colored poster board. Color in each clown's smile and 2 of the noses. The third nose will be the target.

5 When it's time to play the game, hang the poster board on the wall. Each player takes a nose, is blindfolded, and then tries to tape the missing nose on the correct clown.

Electronic Librarians

Browsing up and down the bookshelves in a library is fun, but sometimes you need to find a specific book quickly. Before computers were used in libraries, information for each book was written on three types of index cards in a *card catalog*. These cards were stored alphabetically according to the author, subject, and title of each book. Each card indicated where you could find a certain book in the library.

Today, most libraries have replaced their card catalogs with *computer cataloging programs*. When looking for a book, you type in the author, subject, or title and the computer tells you where the book is located and whether it's been checked out.

Check it out: Has your local or school library replaced its old card catalog with PCs? If so, try finding a book using the computer. Carefully read the options listed on the monitor. Usually, F keys are pressed to move around. Remember to use care when using a library computer and ask a librarian for help if you need it.

Fun & Games

If computer games really get you geared up for fun, you'll have double the excitement making games on your computer to play any time, any place! After you've tried these ideas, strike out on your own and create new games to play with friends and family. Design a board game that relates to a subject you're studying in school. Or, think up a card game about events happening in your neighborhood. Maybe you'll want to combine two games you already know into a whole new game. Whatever you decide, rev up your imagination and have fun!

ILLUSION PUZZLE

×××

Dutch graphic artist M. C. Escher is famous for his optical illusion designs. This puzzle uses his technique of repeated simple, dark shapes as a super way to practice with your computer's Copy and Paste functions.

WHAT YOU NEED

Glue

Cardboard

Scissors

WHAT YOU DO

1 Create a small, simple shape. Add a little detail such as an eye or a mouth.

2 Copy your shape, then Paste several times in a row, side by side so they touch slightly on each side.

3 Copy the row of shapes, then Paste the set below the first row, so it just touches.

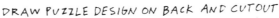

DESIGN A SHAPE

COPY AND PASTE
SIDE BY SIDE FOR
SEVERAL ROWS

PRINT OUT AND
PASTE ON
CARDBOARD

DRAW PUZZLE DESIGN ON BACK AND CUTOUT

4 Add a few details to the white space between the two rows. Add details to one shape, then Copy/Paste them on the other white shapes.

5 Repeat steps 3 – 4, copying and pasting a second set below the first set. Repeat until your drawing area is filled. Print 1 copy.

6 Glue the artwork onto a piece of cardboard. Trim the edges to fit the art. Cut the cardboard into puzzle pieces. Then see if someone can put it back together again.

COMPUTER Q&A

What Is Point Size?

Most software programs let you type words in different sizes. The size of each letter is measured in *points*, abbreviated "pt." As you'd expect, the larger the point size, the larger the letter. But what are they measuring?

Picture the word "Monkey," and think of each letter as a monkey. Some of the monkeys are reaching up high for a banana. These are the capital *M* and *k*. The *o, n,* and *e* are rolled up taking a nap. The *y* is swinging its tail. Measure from the banana-reaching arm to the swinging tail. If it measures 1 inch (2.5 cm), it is said to be 72 points. (See page 135.)

Tic-TAC-BOO

×××

Tic-Tac-Toe has never been such fun! Think of other themes such as the Wild West with cowboys, cactus, or horses for game pieces. Decorate board squares with horseshoes. Yee haw!

WHAT YOU NEED

Colored printer paper

Scissors

Glue stick

Construction paper, 9" (22.5 cm) square

WHAT YOU DO

1 Draw a ghost, making it about 3" × 3" (7.5 cm × 7.5 cm). Add a long rectangular base at its feet so it can stand up.

2 Copy/Paste as many as will fit on your screen. Print out 5 white ghosts and 5 of another color. Cut them out with the bases.

3 Decorate ghosts. Fold bases back for stands.

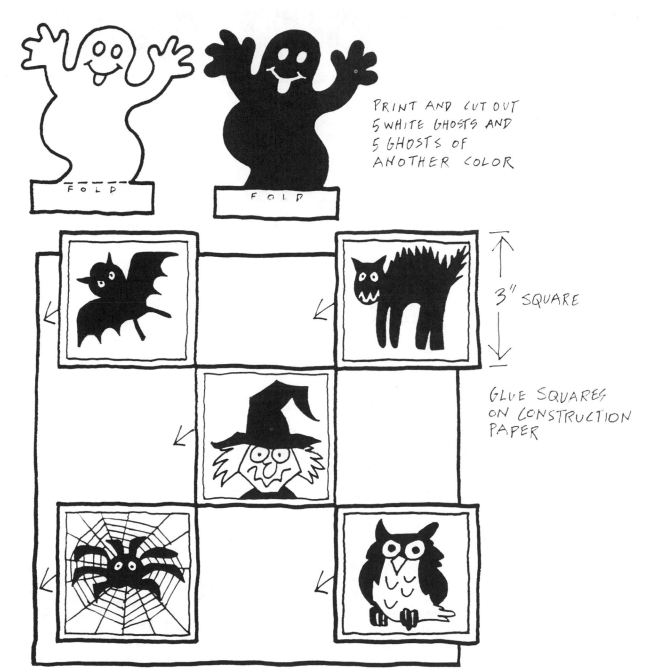

4 To make game board squares: Draw a 3" (7.5 cm) square and decorate with a haunting design. Make a total of 5 squares. Print and cut out.

5 To make the game board: Glue one square in each corner and one in the center of the construction paper.

6 Play like tic-tac-toe, using one color ghost as "X" pieces, and the other as "O's." Take turns placing a ghost on either a decorated or plain square, trying to get 3 of your ghosts in a row.

PRINT AND CUT OUT
5 WHITE GHOSTS AND
5 GHOSTS OF
ANOTHER COLOR

FOLD

FOLD

3" SQUARE

GLUE SQUARES
ON CONSTRUCTION
PAPER

SOUR GRAPES

If you like playing card games, you'll like this game, too. Choose different themes, such as your favorite comic book or computer game characters. Don't forget to include a villain for the card no one wants to get stuck with!

 **WHAT YOU DO**

1 You'll need 10 characters and 1 villain for this game. Plan a theme. For example, choose fruits andvegetables as your theme and have "sour grapes" be the villain.

2 To make cards: Draw a 2" x 3" (5 cm x 7.5 cm) rectangle on the screen. Make 11 same-sized rectangles, and draw a character on each one. Print 2 copies of each card, except the villain.

3 Cut out each card and mix them up.

4 Deal 5 cards to each player, with extras face down in a stack. Players take turns choosing either a new card from the stack or a card from another player. As pairs are formed, put them together on the table. The person holding the villain at the end deals the next hand.

Extra! Extra!

Newspaper offices used to be noisy, frantic places where reporters and editors noisily typed articles on typewriters. When finished, a reporter shouted "Copy!" and a copy boy would take the typed pages to the editor. Editors shouted questions across the room to reporters, who shouted answers back.

With today's computers, newspaper offices are often much quieter places. Reporters type their stories on the silent keyboards of a PC. And with the push of a button, their stories are sent to the computer's memory, ready to be called up by an editor, who makes cuts and changes right on screen! Then the story is set into type electronically.

GRANNY SMITH | LIMEY | STRAW-BERRY TART | BANANA MANA | SQUASH | LEMON AID

$14 · 14 CARROT | ORANG-U-TAN | CHERÍ | SPLIT PEA | CHILLY PEPPER | SOUR GRAPES

DESIGN AND PRINT 2 COPIES OF EACH CARD. USE ONLY ONE VILLAIN CARD →

SLIDING SWITCHEROO

XXXXXXXXXXXXXXXXXXXXXXXXXXXXXXXXXXXXXXXXXXXXXXXXXXXXXXXXXXXXXX

Make several copies of this game board, and challenge your friends to see who can switch the circle and triangle fastest.

WHAT YOU NEED

Scissors

Markers, several colors

WHAT YOU DO

Draw a rectangle, then divide it into 3 top squares and 3 bottom squares. Draw a small square inside 3 squares, a circle in one square, and a triangle in one square. Leave one square empty. Decorate game board with a border. Print 1 copy.

GAME PIECES:

GAME BOARD:

LEAVE ONE SQUARE BLANK

2 Draw 3 small squares, 1 circle, and 1 triangle, the same sizes as those on the game board. Print and cut out shapes. These are your game pieces.

3 Match game pieces on top of their shapes on the board. Without any diagonal moves, switch the positions of the circle and triangle. Move 1 shape at a time into an empty square. Count how many moves it takes you.

TO PLAY: MOVE SHAPES AS SHOWN

SWITCHED

TO WIN: SWITCH CIRCLE AND SQUARE

Computer Board Games

Ask some grown-ups what their favorite board games were. Did they mention playing Monopoly® or Scrabble® at the kitchen table for hours on end?

Today you can play Monopoly® and many, many other games right on your computer! Plays are made by clicking and dragging game pieces with your mouse, and cards can even speak to you when you choose one. Many games also incorporate computer skills, such as using a mouse quickly and accurately. Others use animation and time dead-lines for fast-paced plays.

Why Are Many Games on CD-ROM?

You may wonder why so many games and computerized books come on CDs instead of floppies. Well, CDs can hold almost 450 times the information a floppy disk can hold! Most computerized games and books have complicated graphics and sound effects, requiring more memory than a floppy has. Some games, however, do not require as much memory, so they can fit on a floppy disk.

A Printer's Dream-Come-True

The printing industry has been revolutionized by computers. Previously, the layout of a page was arranged by cutting pieces and pasting them together in the desired format. Pictures, their captions, headlines, and copy were pasted in place by a designer, and the resulting page layout was photographed. It was painstaking work that took a lot of time and patience.

Today, computers eliminate the need for scissors and glue. Items can be moved around the computer screen effortlessly. Rulers along the screen show the user exactly where the item is on a printed page. Color can be altered and type faces changed, just by pushing a few buttons. This was only a dream a few years ago!

Be an investigative reporter: Interview a grown-up or family member about how computers have changed the workplace. You'll soon discover that just about every industry has a use for computers. Engineers use them to draw blue prints, librarians use them to keep track of books, and auto mechanics use computerized equipment to test car safety!

GETTING THE POINT

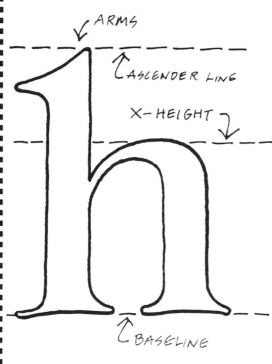

ARMS

ASCENDER LINE

X-HEIGHT

BASELINE

Here's a quick point size chart to help you figure out how large to make your type. Remember, you need to measure from the very top of the letters (arms) to the very bottom (tails).

> 9 points = 1/8 inch (2.5 mm)
>
> 18 points = 1/4 inch (5 mm)
>
> 36 points = 1/2 inch (1 cm)
>
> 72 points = 1 inch (2.5 cm)

For a more detailed chart, make your own list of sizes. Start with the smallest point size your computer can make, then create different sizes. What is the largest point size your computer can type? Are you sure? Sometimes there are more choices than meet the eye. Look in your software manual under "font size" to see if there are any tricks to making larger type.

DESCENDER LINE

TAILS

0   1/8"   1/4"   1/2"   1"
9 POINTS 18 POINTS   36 POINTS   72 POINTS

FISHING FOR AN ANSWER

Here's a game that's fun to play — and good addition practice, too! Or, learn Spanish or another language, by writing a Spanish word on each fish, and making a matching card with its English translation.

WHAT YOU NEED

- Colored printer paper
- Scissors
- Paper clips
- Long stick, string
- Small magnet

DECORATE, PRINT AND CUT OUT NUMBERED PLAYING CARDS

ATTACH PAPER CLIP

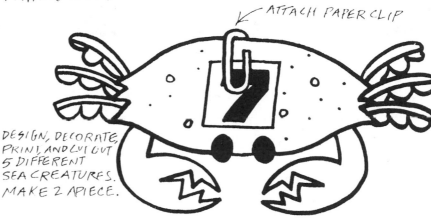

DESIGN, DECORATE, PRINT, AND CUT OUT 5 DIFFERENT SEA CREATURES. MAKE 2 APIECE.

WHAT YOU DO

1 To make numbered playing cards: Draw 10 2" x 3" (5 cm x 7.5 cm) rectangles. Type one number (0 through 9) on each card. Decorate, print, and cut out.

2 Make 10 game pieces by drawing 5 different sea creatures such as large fish, crabs, starfish, or lobsters. Make 2 of each creature and type one number, 0 through 9, on each fish. Print on brightly colored paper. Cut out each piece and slip a paper clip on it.

3 To make the bait, draw a worm, print, and cut out. Make a small hole in the center of its body.

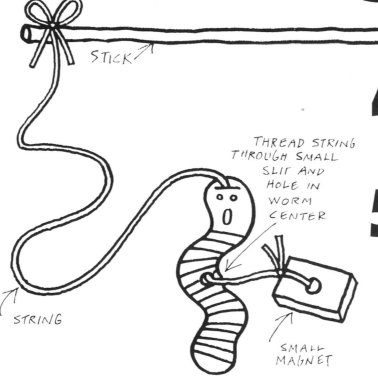

STICK

STRING

THREAD STRING THROUGH SMALL SLIT AND HOLE IN WORM CENTER

SMALL MAGNET

4 To make the fishing pole, tie string to one end of a stick. Thread the worm onto the string and tie this end to the magnet.

5 Place the paper-clipped fish on the floor. Stack the number cards face down in a pile, then choose two cards. Add the number on each card and with the fishing pole, "catch" the fish with the correct answer. If the answer has two numbers (such as "10"), catch two fish ("1" and "0"). Return fish to floor after your turn.

Safety Tips for Saving

Have you ever been working on the computer when the power went out because of a storm? Has someone ever accidentally unplugged the computer while you were using it? If this has happened, you know that all your work is gone, because it was not saved to the hard drive. So, whenever you open a new document, go to the File menu and choose Save As. Then you can name it and make it permanent. Now any work you add will be in the short-term memory, or RAM, until you tell the computer to store it by choosing Save. Every time you go to the Save command, a little more information is saved. Remember this rule: *SOS: Save Often Silly.*

Save As is also useful when you want to make a copy of a document, add changes, but keep the original intact.

See for yourself: Open a new document. Go to the Save As command and name your document "Letter to Grandma." Now type a letter, telling her what you are learning with your computer. Remember, SOS. When finished, choose Save one last time. Okay, now all your hard work can be used when you type a letter to your aunt. With the first letter still on the screen, go to the Save As command. Name this document "Letter to Aunt." Now add to, or change, Grandma's letter. This variation becomes your Aunt's letter, but Grandma's original is still saved, too.

File	
New Folder	⌘N
Open	⌘O
Close	⌘W
Get Info	⌘I
Save	⌘S
Save As...	
Find...	⌘F
Find Again	⌘G
Page Setup...	
Print	

WEARABLE ART

Make a lucky fishing visor or create your own line of fashion, making accessories to match your wardrobe. Draw jewelry patterns and decorations, then add color, ribbons, and glitter for pizzazz. Think of a name for your jewelry line; then make display cards for your creations.

LUCKY FISHING VISOR

You're bound to catch the "big one" with this hat on your head! Decorate with your favorite story characters, animals, or even caricatures of your friends!

WHAT YOU NEED

Markers, several colors

Glue stick

Scissors

Plastic hat visor

 **WHAT YOU DO**

1 Draw an underwater scene. Include your favorite sea creatures and other decorations. Print 1 copy, color, and cut out the creatures as separate pieces.

2 Glue pieces to the visor. Be sure to completely coat pieces and rub them down well.

3 Go fishing and hum some favorite tunes!

Coughing Computers!

Computers don't really cough, of course, but they do get viruses. A computer virus is a software program that a skilled but mischievous person writes to hurt a computer. It works much the way a real virus does when you catch a cold from sharing a glass with a sneezing friend. In this case, viruses are passed through infected disks, and across networks and modems, too. A virus can be minor, only slowing your computer's speed. However, there are some viruses destructive enough to eat up your programs! To protect your computer from viruses, you can install *anti-virus software*, available at your local software store.

SPORTS PIN

✿✿✿

Choose your favorite sport and create a pin to wear on your jacket or your cap. Make a pin with your team logo or a soccer ball, football, basketball, or tennis racket.

WHAT YOU NEED

Safety pin

Scissors

Markers, several colors

Glue stick

Tape

Poster board

WHAT YOU DO

1 Draw a logo or some sport equipment, about 2" (5 cm) high. Print 1 copy.

2 Color and glue to poster board. Cut out.

3 Tape a safety pin to back of poster board, and pin to your shirt or cap. Or, pin to a computer-created greeting card and give as a gift.

DESIGN, PRINT OUT,
AND GLUE TO
POSTER BOARD.

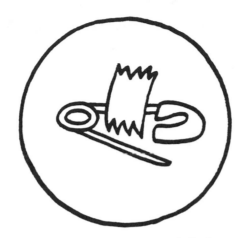

TAPE A SAFETY PIN
TO BACK SIDE.

DESIGN DIFFERENT-SHAPED SPORT PINS

NEW, NEWER, NEWEST!

Computerized Cars

Believe it or not, most of the cars we drive today are made with the help of computer-automated robots. You may not realize it, but computers are also found inside today's auto-mobiles. Various parts such as the engine, brakes, exhaust control, and suspension, are adjusted by computers to make an auto run efficiently and safely.

BEADED PAPER NECKLACE

Create a one-of-a-kind necklace to wear for special occasions. For large beads, roll paper over a pencil and string with yarn. Or, tie ribbons between beads for a fringed effect.

Glue stick

Toothpick

Sewing needle

Thread, about 20"
(50 cm) long

Scissors

Markers, several colors

 WHAT YOU DO

DECORATE TRIANGLES, PRINT AND CUT OUT.

1 Draw a large rectangle and divide it into long, narrow triangles, as shown. Decorate each triangle and print.

2 Cut out each triangle and color one side. Or, print out shapes on colored paper.

3 Beginning at the wide end, roll each triangle onto a toothpick. Glue down triangle tip and slide off the toothpick. Make about 30 of these.

4 Ask a grown-up to help you thread a needle, and string the paper beads together for a necklace.

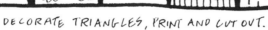

BEGIN AT WIDE END—ROLL EACH TRIANGLE ON TOOTHPICK

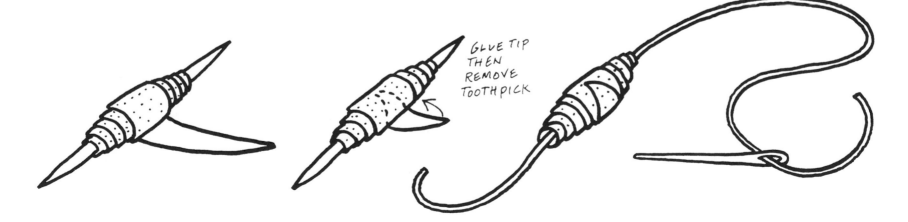

GLUE TIP THEN REMOVE TOOTHPICK

Ticker Tape Parades

Years ago, the New York Stock Exchange sent stock price information across the country on a device called a ticker tape machine. At the end of every day, the tape — long rolls of narrow paper strips — were swept up and set aside. Then, when a parade was held for heroes, veterans, or presidents, people would throw the long strands of ticker tape from windows as the parade marched past.

In 1962, the last parade to actually use real ticker tape was held for astronaut John Glenn, the first American to orbit the Earth.

Today, stock prices appear on computer screens because ticker tape can't handle the amount of business now done on the stock exchange. Even though computer technology has brought an end to ticker tape parades, it hasn't, of course, brought an end to celebrations. Today, people toss something somewhat similar to honor heroes — shredded computer printouts!

How Many Programs Are Too Many?

Your hard disk acts as a large filing cabinet where your work is stored. The larger your hard disk, the larger the filing cabinet. If you try to install too many software programs on a hard disk without enough space available, your computer won't accept the programs. (Eventually, even a big filing cabinet runs out of room!) When this happens you can either delete files you no longer use (like tossing out some old papers) or buy a larger hard disk.

If you have very little hard disk space, sometimes while working on a document, you may not be able to "save" because there isn't enough room. If this happens, try saving your document to a floppy disk instead.

NEW, NEWER, NEWEST!

Recycle Those Old Computers and Printers

Is your family's old computer or printer collecting dust while you use a newer model? Wait! Don't throw the old one out. Many schools, libraries, and nonprofit businesses would greatly appreciate your old, but working computer or printer. If it is still in working shape, donate it to a good cause.

Do you know someone who would like to learn a little about computers, but doesn't own one? Well, older models are great to learn on. Just put a big red bow on it and give it to Grandma or your neighbor for a birthday surprise! Attach a homemade card that says you will give computer lessons, too! Welcoming someone to the computer age is a terrific gift!

DESIGNER HAIR COMB

This comb will look great using any favorite design. Decorate with flowers, butterflies, music notes, or roller skates. Anything goes!

Hair comb

Colored printer paper

Scissors

Glue stick

Garbage bag twist tie

Ribbon

1 Draw a rectangle on your computer that measures the width of your hair comb, about 1/2" (1 cm) high. Type your name in the shape. Print 1 copy and cut out.

2 Draw the outline of a flower and another identical flower, a bit larger. Draw a third flower, larger than the second. Print 1 copy of the flowers and cut out.

3 Glue your name on the comb.

4 Stack the flowers on each other with the largest on the bottom. Cut 2 slots in the center of all three and thread a twist tie through. Twist onto the hair comb.

5 Poke a hole in the rectangle and thread the ribbons through.

TYPE NAME IN A RECTANGLE AND PRINT OUT

PRINT ONE COPY OF DIFFERENT-SIZED FLOWERS AND CUT OUT

STACK FLOWERS AND MAKE 2 SLITS THROUGH CENTERS

INSERT A TWIST TIE THROUGH SLITS

MAKE HOLES AND TIE ON RIBBONS

ATTACH FLOWER TO COMB

 # PAPIER-MACHE BANGLES

WHAT YOU NEED

Poster board

Newspaper

Masking tape

Scissors

Papier-Mache recipe
(see page 151)

Let your creativity really fly! Design a whole line of papier-mache bracelets, using American Indian or African motifs.

WHAT YOU DO

1 Draw 2 long rectangles, about 2" (5 cm) high, on the screen.

2 Decorate 1 rectangle with an American Indian or African motif. Copy and paste the design several times inside the rectangle for a bracelet pattern.

3 Decorate the other rectangle with another design, perhaps creating a black background for your image.

4 Print 2 copies and cut out the rectangles.

5 For the bracelet, cut a piece of poster board 9" x 1" (22.5 cm x 2.5 cm). Wrap around your wrist so it fits properly (it should be a bit large). Tape the ends together.

6 Follow instructions for making papier-mache. Tear newspaper into 1"-wide (2.5 cm) strips and dip into the paste, one strip at a time.

7 Remove excess paste from the strips with your fingers, then wind the strips over the bracelet. Make several layers over the poster board.

8 Dip your designed strips into the paste. With design showing, drape strips over outside of bracelet, folding excess to the inside. Cut off excess paper, and let dry overnight. Add color with tempera or puffy paints, if you wish.

AFRICAN DESIGN

PUEBLO INDIAN DESIGN

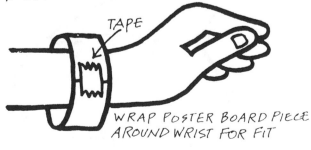

TAPE

WRAP POSTER BOARD PIECE AROUND WRIST FOR FIT

WIND PASTE-DIPPED STRIPS AROUND THE BRACELETS

WRAP PASTE-DIPPED DESIGN STRIPS ON OUTSIDE OF BRACELET

PAPIER-MACHE PASTE RECIPE

WHAT YOU NEED

- 1/2 cup (125 ml) flour
- 1 tablespoon (15 ml) salt
- 1 cup (250 ml) warm water

WHAT YOU DO

Mix flour and salt in a bowl. Add the warm water to the flour and salt mixture, and mix with your hands until it feels like a thin milkshake.

HIDDEN SECRET KEY CHAIN

Keep a special picture in this hidden secret key chain. Your picture or drawing can be of anything or anyone — even your lovable pet! Or, it can keep a number you need to remember — like your Mom's office number.

WHAT YOU NEED

Glue stick
Scissors
Markers, several colors
Yarn

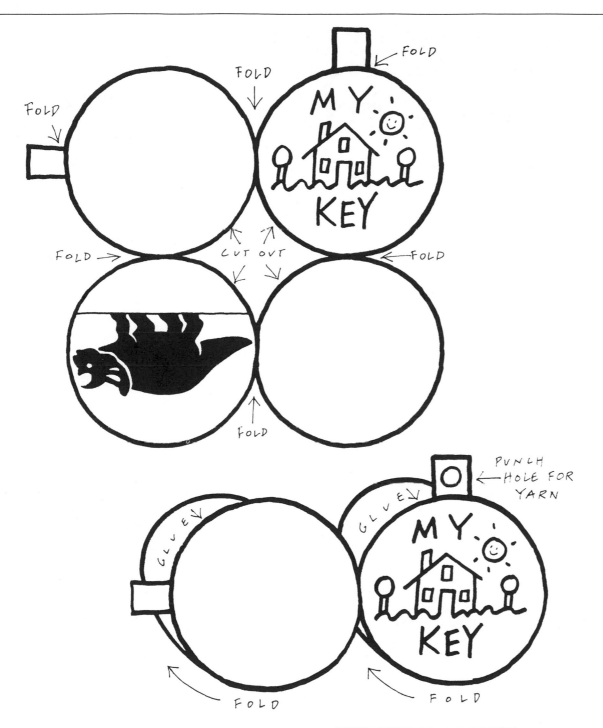

1 Draw four 2" (5 cm) circles, two with tabs. Your circles should touch.

2 In the upper right circle, type your initials or nickname.

3 In the lower left circle, draw a design or use a piece of clip art (see page 93). Because the front will be folded upward, draw your design upside down.

4 Print 1 copy and cut out. Cut away the diamond-shaped white space in center of design.

5 Fold the lower 2 circles upward, and glue unprinted sides together. Color your key chain charm. Fold the left circle forward over the right. Fold back tab on side to close the locket.

6 Reinforce top tab with some clear tape; poke a small hole in the top tab and string with a piece of yarn, or strong elastic band.

NEW, NEWER, NEWEST!

Ease on Down the Road

Have you heard of the *information superhighway*? You may know it by its other name, the Internet. This global system connects millions of computers, much the way roads and highways connect towns and cities. Computers are linked by regular phone lines, fiber optical networks, and microwave transmissions. Large organizations use computers to store huge amounts of information, and the Internet opens these systems so users thousands of miles away can get information from them. Your school or home computer can be linked to the Internet, too. All you need is the proper software, a telephone line, and a modem.

Imagine you have to write a report about a NASA moon landing. You could get on the Internet, link to NASA's computer files, and view photos of the landing — right on your computer screen. You could even see interviews with the astronauts!

INDEX

A

KIDS CAN! BOOKS
FROM WILLIAMSON PUBLISHING

The following *Kids Can!* books are each 160-176 pages, fully illustrated, trade paper, 11 x 8 ¹/2, $12.95 US. Please see last page for ordering information.

THE KIDS' SCIENCE BOOK
Creative Experiences for Hands-On Fun
by Robert Hirschfeld and Nancy White

. . . .

Winner of the Parents' Choice Gold Award!

THE KIDS' MULTICULTURAL ART BOOK
Art & Craft Experiences from Around the World
by Alexandra M. Terzian

. . . .

Winner of the Parents' Choice Gold Award!

Winner of Benjamin Franklin Best Juvenile Nonfiction Award!

KIDS MAKE MUSIC!
Clapping and Tapping from Bach to Rock
by Avery Hart and Paul Mantell

KIDS & WEEKENDS!
Creative Ways to Make Special Days
by Avery Hart and Paul Mantell

. . . .

American Bookseller Pick-of-the Lists

KIDS' CRAZY CONCOCTIONS
50 Mysterious Mixtures for Art & Craft Fun
by Jill F. Hauser

Children's Book-of-the-Month Club Main Selection

THE LITTLE HANDS ART BOOK
Exploring Arts & Crafts with
2- to 6-Year-Olds
Judy Press

. . . .

Winner of the Oppenheim Toy Portfolio Best Book Award!

EcoArt!
Earth-Friendly Art & Craft Experiences for 3- to 9-Year-Olds
by Laurie Carlson

KIDS COOK!
Fabulous Food for the Whole Family
by Sarah Williamson and Zachary Williamson

THE KIDS' WILDLIFE BOOK
Exploring Animal Worlds through Indoor/Outdoor Crafts & Experiences
by Warner Shedd

KIDS' GARDEN!
The Anytime, Anyplace Guide to Sowing & Growing Fun
by Avery Hart and Paul Mantell

HANDS AROUND THE WORLD
365 Creative Ways to Build Cultural Awareness & Global Respect
by Susan Milord

THE KIDS' MULTICULTURAL COOKBOOK
Food & Fun Around the World
by Deanna Cook

. . . .

Winner of the Parents' Choice Gold Award!

THE KIDS' NATURE BOOK
365 Indoor/Outdoor Activities and Experiences
by Susan Milord

KIDS CREATE!
Art & Craft Experiences for
3- to 9-Year-Olds
by Laurie Carlson

. . . .

Parents Magazine Parents' Pick

KIDS LEARN AMERICA!
Bringing Geography to Life with People, Places, & History
by Patricia Gordon and Reed C. Snow

. . . .

American Bookseller Pick-of-the Lists

ADVENTURES IN ART
Art & Craft Experiences for
7- to 14-Year-Olds
by Susan Milord